Salesman's
Complete
Model Letter
Handbook

SALESMAN'S COMPLETE MODEL LETTER HANDBOOK

Ferd Nauheim

PARKER PUBLISHING COMPANY, INC.
WEST NYACK, NEW YORK

PRINTED IN THE UNITED STATES OF AMERICA

B & P

Dedication

To Bea, who gamely shared nearly a year of lost weekends while this book was being written, and who helped in so many ways.

A Treasury of Ideas for Effective Letters

This book heralds a new, dynamic approach to selling that has proven its immense effectiveness. The letters and letter systems in the pages that follow have blazed the trail to record-smashing sales. For example, you will read the fine detail of an appointment-winning letter and phone combination that tripled the number of appointments salesmen were getting in office after office across the United States. The same combination has been adopted by salesmen in a variety of businesses and localities, and each has found it amazingly successful.

The biggest sales and the most enduring relationships with good customers are built on ideas. One of the many valuable and exciting benefits in this book is the wealth of stimulating sales ideas you will find in the model letters. You will find ideas that open the doors to new customers... ideas that recover lost accounts... ideas that convert casual buyers to important and constant customers... ideas that change complainers to friends.

In many cases, salesmen and sales managers will be able to use letters in this book with little or no change. But even where a complete change is required to fit a particular set of circumstances, the model letters point the way... show how your own letter should be written... make it quick and easy for you to take the letter action needed.

There are many things letters can do that salesmen cannot do and these will be revealed to you ... will become part of your everyday selling technique... as you read.

Chapters 15 through 19 help to solve many of the biggest problems sales managers face. The scores of model letters in these chapters go well beyond offering sales managers time-saving tools to handle specific situations. They enable a busy sales manager to see through the surface of many a vexing problem right to the heart of the matter ... to adopt creative and effective mental attitudes ... to help him build a stronger, more loyal sales force.

This is a book to be read through thoroughly and to be used as a ready, dependable reference from then on. It is a book that will go to work for you whenever written contact with customers and prospects is indicated. It is a book to browse through whenever sales and your spirits are in a slump. It is a book to check through when in need of a powerful sales idea.

Table of Contents

Salesman's
Complete
Model Letter
Handbook

1

Letters Following a Sale

The letter you send after a sale has been made is an expected business courtesy. It is easy enough to dash off a note expressing your thanks. These two elements...the fact that such letters are expected, and the ease of simply saying thanks...constitute a challenge.

Your objective is to get the greatest impact out of every letter you write.

When you write a thank you letter after a sale, therefore, make every effort to put into that letter evidence of the full depth of your appreciation...your desire to serve...your personality...your understanding of the listener and:

PUT YOURSELF IN THE PACKAGE

Use your letter of thanks to let a customer know that your interest in him didn't end with the decision to buy. Getting the money or the signature is half of the sale you are capable of making. The other half consists of cementing that relationship in a manner that paves the way to future business, or, if the item purchased is probably a "once only" transaction, such as a home, giving the customer the desire to refer you to friends.

Tell the customer that you are part of the package he bought.

Dear Mr. Beeman,

I deeply appreciate the business you gave me yesterday. Your signing the order is only a beginning because I'm making it my responsibility to see to it that it is executed accurately and promptly.

1

And after delivery I'll be checking to be certain that you get the utmost of satisfaction and service.

Many thanks . . .

———————

Dear Mr. Grisscom,

You bought me, too.

Yesterday, when you placed that fine order you bought me, too.

I am going to make a point of getting in touch with you from time to time just to be sure that there are no problems or questions. And it is my hope that you always will feel free to call me if you need help of any kind.

My sincerest thanks.

Cordially,

———————

Dear Mr. Frayter,

You and Mrs. Frayter gave me a lot yesterday, and I am most grateful.

You gave me much more than some business. You gave me your confidence. That means a great deal to me.

Times and circumstances change. The decisions that were made at our meeting yesterday appear to be, in my judgment, ideal at this time. You and I will both be watching the progress of your program and you can be certain that I'll be in touch with you from time to time to review it . . . to determine if altering conditions may possibly dictate the need for change.

Please call me if you ever have any questions or want my ideas, suggestions or help.

I look forward to future meetings with you. Please give my best regards to Mrs. Frayter.

Cordially,

LETTERS TO STORE CUSTOMERS

If you are a retail salesman working in a store, you can use letters with great effectiveness in your efforts to develop a group of loyal customers who will come back to you whenever they need the merchandise you sell. Your thank you letters can build that desire.

Dear Mr. Jenner,

It was a genuine pleasure for me to serve you yesterday. I hope I'll have that pleasure repeated frequently.

As we receive shipments of new merchandise, there will be some occasions when I'll see something that may impress me as being particularly suitable for you. When I do, I will take the liberty of calling you or dropping you a line.

In the meantime if you, or any of your friends or business associates, are in need of anything I can supply, I'll be delighted to have the opportunity.

Cordially,

———————

Dear Mrs. Procket,

Many thanks for the purchase you made yesterday. Working with you was most enjoyable.

When delivery is made and the new furniture is in place, I hope you'll be as delighted and as proud as I think you will be. If just the right placement creates any problems, by all means give me a ring. I'll be more than happy to come to your home to help in any way I can.

Once you are happy with the arrangement you may see the need to fill in with some occasional pieces or accessories and I'm sure that we can find just the right items that will harmonize perfectly.

I look forward to seeing you and working with you again.

Sincerely,

———————

Dear Mrs. Ganes,

It was so nice having the pleasure of serving you yesterday. Thank you for giving me the opportunity.

I do hope that the gift you chose is well received. Helping in the selection of gifts has become my favorite occupation . . . I enjoy it so.

Whenever you need a gift for any occasion, I'll consider it a real privilege if you'll call on me. If time is pressing, just phone; tell me your budget and the type of gift you have in mind and leave the hunting to me. That's the way I work with many of our customers.

Sincerely,

———————

Dear Mr. Harrold,

I checked with our service and delivery departments just now. Your handsome new television console will be delivered and installed Wednesday afternoon, just as promised.

My warmest thanks, Mr. Harrold, for making the purchase through me. It was thoughtful of you to come equipped with that drawing of your den and the exact measurements of the space. The set should fit in handsomely.

Even though our installation people are expert at their work, I'd like to drop by one evening on my way home from work to check your reception myself. You have a remarkably fine set, and I want to be certain that you are getting the utmost enjoyment from it.

Before I come, I'll give you a ring to make sure that it will not inconvenience you.

Thanks again.

Cordially,

SAYING THANKS TO CAR AND HOME BUYERS

The larger the purchase, the greater your effort must be to lift your thank you letter many notches above the ordinary. While the man who bought a new suit won't be surprised to get a thank you letter, he won't be offended if it is absent. But the man who makes a purchase that represents a large sum of money, fully expects written thanks and your letter should do more than express gratitude. Rare is the individual who makes a major purchase who doesn't harbor some misgivings. Your letter should reinforce his decision to buy.

Dear Mr. Bellsame,

How many miles have you put on the new car?

That's the only fault I have been able to find with it . . . it hurts to get out from behind the wheel of a car that is such a joy to drive.

When you bring your car in for the routine checks and servicing, you'll find the men in our service department wonderful people. They are as interested in your total satisfaction as I am.

I am very grateful that you dealt with me, Mr. Bellsame. Look for me in the showroom or give me a ring any time I can do anything for you. And if anyone you know gets particularly jealous of that beautiful car of yours, just tell him to see me.

Thanks again and many miles of happy driving.

Cordially,

————

Dear Mr. and Mrs. Hartsone,

Congratulations and my heartfelt thanks.

I know how impatient you must be to move into your lovely new home. That was a major decision you made yesterday and I am confident that you'll always be delighted that you made the choice you did.

It was a warm and enjoyable experience working with the two of you. I'll always be grateful for the opportunity and for your trust and confidence.

You can be sure that I'll conscientiously follow through on all the details and will let you know promptly when the settlement date has been set.

If there's anything I can do in the meantime, by all means call me.

Thanks once more. I'll see you soon and look forward to it.

Cordially,

THANK YOU FOR THE CONTRACT

When you have worked long and hard to win the award of a contract, you have every reason to be jubilant when it comes through. The buyer usually knows the pleasure the winning of the contract will give you. Buyers are human. When they agree to do business with you by putting their signatures to agreements, they relish evidence of the gratification they have created. Don't hold back. Give your new customer that satisfaction. You are human too and if you reveal your human qualities, you will give your new customer added reasons to like and to trust you. All of us feel closer to those who display enthusiasm and warmth . . . we have the impulse to want to do still more for them. We have greater faith in the people we like.

Dear Mr. Mallrak,

Although I said it on the phone when you called to tell me I had been awarded the contract, I just had to obey the impulse to say thank you in writing.

There are several layers to the great pleasure the news gave me. On top is the happiness of knowing that the waiting and hoping are over and I won. But of even greater depth and substance is the anticipation of a long relationship with you as we go to work. I know how stimulating, rewarding and enjoyable that will be, and I'm eager to start.

I'll be on hand promptly for our Tuesday morning meeting.

Much appreciation.

Cordially,

Dear Mr. Sloats,

Thanks for a grand homecoming.

While traveling home from our meeting I did a complete mental review of the questions you had raised and the answers I had given. When you said you would let me know I, frankly, was disappointed for I had hoped to come home with the order. The proposition seemed so right for you.

You can picture my reaction when I came to my office this morning and found your letter of agreement.

Now I can really prove all the things I promised, Mr. Sloats. You can be sure that I'll give my fullest energy to doing so.

Many thanks.

Cordially,

————————

Dear Mr. Young,

Even though we are many miles apart, I wondered if you heard the popping of champagne corks and the singing in the streets.

Your letter and contract arrived this morning . . . just five minutes ago . . . and I want you to know how deeply grateful I am.

As soon as I have finished writing this letter, I shall make travel arrangements to come to you next week as you suggested. It will be grand to see you again and to get started on the project.

Gratefully,

————————

Dear Mr. Randor,

What great news.

I just was advised that you have included us in your advertising schedule for next year. Thank you so very much.

Your job is an immensely difficult one, and I fully appreciate how complex it is for you to fit something fresh and new into your budget and your schedules. But after our last meeting, I confess, I sensed that you saw the unusual values we offer and had high hopes that you'd fit us in.

I'll be on my toes watching for your material to give it silk glove handling.

My heartiest gratitude. I'll be by to see you in the near future.

Cordially,

There are some occasions when the awarding of a contract represents a particularly difficult decision on the part of the buyer. The more difficult the decision, the more you can be certain that he is likely to have doubts and fears about his judgment. Support his decision. Let him know the fullness of your understanding of his problems. Give him reason, at the outset of your relationship, to feel that he did the right thing.

Dear Mr. Preston,

I am delighted. The whole company is delighted.

You and I have had many meetings, and I knew that each one brought us closer to doing business. At the same time I have been fully aware of the problems and the pressures involved when a firm like yours changes from a long-term supplier to a new one.

In bringing about the change you have put your experience, knowledge and judgment on the line. My company and I are completely aware of that and you can be satisfied that we will spare nothing to justify your decision.

You have always had my fullest respect. Now, in addition, you have my total dedication, loyalty and warmest gratitude.

Sincerely,

The Opening of New Wholesale Accounts

It is a start. When a retailer or a jobber places his initial order with you, the natural hope and expectation is that he will become a continuing buyer and an important one. Your thank you letter, therefore, should display your readiness to serve and to cooperate, in addition to your appreciation.

Dear Mr. Whittley,

I have much to thank you for.

Thank you for the order . . . for the check . . . for starting to do business with us . . . but, most of all, for being so pleasant to deal with.

Your order will be processed and shipped just as quickly as possible. I've also arranged to have some handsome new display material included. You'll find, as so many of our customers do, that the merchandise will move quickly, so I anticipate that we'll be hearing from you again quite soon.

My next trip to your city is scheduled for the fifteenth of next month. It will be a great pleasure to see you.

Cordially.

––––––––––

Dear Mr. Royce,

I even thanked the letter carrier.

This morning's mail brought me that fine order from you, and I wish I could be there in person to tell you how gratified I am that you made the decision to work with us.

You can be confident that I will do everything in my power to give you continuing reason to be glad you decided to handle our merchandise. I'll be on hand next Thursday morning to conduct that training session with your sales force.

Your initial order is being processed now and will be shipped before the day is over.

My sincerest thanks.

Cordially,

New Business from Old Customers

Thank you letters should by no means be confined to new accounts. When established customers favor you with unusually large orders or renew an existing contract, you have valid reason to express your feelings. Since they are old customers and your relationship probably has gone beyond the area of buyer and seller, write your letter in a manner that reflects the ties that have been established.

Dear Bob,

How big . . . how loud . . . how clear can a fellow say THANK YOU.

Over the years you have given me many fine orders, but the one that came in the mail this morning made my head swim.

An order like that touches off many reactions. Foremost, I'm so very happy for the warm friendship you've given me. Secondly, I'm so delighted that my firm has been able to satisfy you so well . . . today's order is testimony to that. Thirdly, I'm so pleased that your business is growing at such a pace that an order of this size is possible.

With utmost gratitude . . .

Dear George,

What a nice order. Many, many thanks.

When your orders come in I always get a double measure of pleasure from them. It is nice to get business, of course, but your orders are like letters from home.

Thanks for being the kind of a person who is capable of giving me that warm feeling whenever I hear from you.

My best . . .

Dear Pete,

A sincere and hearty thanks, Pete, for the renewal of the contract.

You've been wonderfully loyal over the years, but my expectation of your renewal doesn't diminish my gratitude when your renewal arrives.

I hope that your business is continuing to flourish and that you and your fine family are enjoying good health. Give my best to Marge.

Cordially,

In Summary . . . .

Your letters of appreciation for business given can pave the way to continuing and increased business if you will put some extra thought and understanding into the composition of them. Your thank you letters should . . .

1. Demonstrate that you have put yourself in the package.
2. Increase the desire for retail store customers to come back to you.
3. Give retail buyers of substantial items the conviction that they made the right decision.
4. Let businessmen who have awarded you contracts savor the full dimensions of your appreciation.
5. Express your understanding of the need for justification when a difficult buying decision has been made.
6. Show your readiness to serve when new wholesale accounts have been opened.
7. Radiate the warmth of a long association when an established customer gives you a large order or renews an existing agreement.

2

Letters Following
a Refusal to Buy

A presentation to a new prospect represents an investment. You have invested time, effort, thought and, in many cases, travel expense. If you don't make a sale, you still may be able to realize dividends and profits from your investment.

Do the Unexpected

It is not unusual for people to receive pleasant letters of thanks when they start doing business with a new company. It is most unusual, however, for anyone to get a gracious letter from a salesman they turned down. Salesmen who do pleasant *unusual* things are remembered.

When you made the presentation that failed to result in a sale, you did succeed in making your company known . . . you made the prospect familiar with your merchandise and services . . . you made yourself known. Even though the answer was negative, the time may come when altered circumstances might lead that prospect to a buying decision. At such a time the salesman who made a lasting impression by doing the unexpected stands an excellent chance of being the man who gets the order. The same elements prevail if the prospect who said "No," has occasion to refer a friend or business acquaintance to someone in your field.

And thanking the man who turned you down is so easy.

Dear Mr. Daniels,

One of the things I like most about my work is that even when I don't make a sale, I often make a friend.

I came away from our meeting yesterday with the warm feeling that I had found a new friend. Thank you so much for giving me reason to feel that way.

Cordially,

————————

Dear Mr. Peels,

Although my visit with you yesterday resulted in "no sale," I sincerely appreciate your willingness to hear my proposal.

My real regret was that I didn't bring you an idea that, in your estimation, had genuine benefits for you. Perhaps next time . . . now that I know you, your thoughts and desires . . . I will come closer to the target.

Cordially,

————————

Dear Mr. Acker,

Thanks for what you gave me yesterday.

You gave me some of your valuable time. You gave me your courteous attention. You gave me the opportunity to tell my story.

Although my suggestions didn't fit your needs at this time, I hope that I will have the pleasure of seeing you on other occasions with other ideas.

Cordially,

Pave the Way for Future Calls

There are frequent occasions when a refusal to buy is simply a refusal to buy *now*. The first important step has been taken. The prospective buyer has met you and knows what you offer. The things you heard and observed have given you clues as to how a more successful presentation may be made the next time you call.

Dear Mr. Grace,

Thank you, Mr. Grace. You gave me something yesterday and I value it.

True, you turned down the proposition that I offered, but you considerately detailed your reasons for doing so. They were sound reasons and I thoroughly respect your decision. It was right.

At the same time you gave me a depth of understanding about your methods of operation and your merchandising practices that fired my imagination. As a result I've started work on an idea that dovetails with your concepts. As soon as I have it polished to my own satisfaction, I'll be back.

Cordially,

————————

Dear Mr. Best,

To quote General MacArthur, "I shall return."

I enjoyed meeting you and the enjoyment was not watered down by your decision. After leaving your office yesterday, I did a good deal of thinking about things you told me concerning your company and about the various ways in which my own company might fit your needs and your thinking.

I shall return.

Cordially,

————————

Dear Mr. Tuppell,

Thanks for saying "No," so pleasantly.

I enjoyed meeting you and you gave me reason to hope that the time will come when we will work together.

Now that I have a fuller understanding of your buying schedules, you can be sure I'll be back to see you well before you have committed yourself fully for next season. When I do come back, it will be with many new items and merchandising ideas.

In the meantime, if there is anything you might want from me, your collect call or telegram will be welcomed.

Sincerely,

OFFER SOMETHING HE WANTS

If the failing presentation brought to light something you can do that the prospect probably wants, make the offer of extra service impressive. You have several choices. While you are with the prospect you can discuss the idea ... you can phone him about it the next day ... you can drop in, hoping he can see you, to make the offer ... or, you can write a letter.

Bringing it up while you are with him diminishes the importance of the thought, and you are presenting it while he is in a negative frame of mind. Phoning the next day may be effective, but you may catch him at a time when he has other matters on his mind and you may not win his full understanding or interest. Dropping in may be offensive if you pick a bad moment. A letter, however, can be read when he can give it full attention ... he can show it to others in his organization ... he can keep it as a record of your offer ... the fact that it is in writing gives him greater confidence in the dependability of the terms.

Dear Mr. Lloyd,

It was good of you to see me yesterday. Sale or no sale, I enjoyed meeting you.

When I returned to my office I discussed our meeting with our general manager. I had an idea I think you'll welcome, and he agreed to go along with it.

You expressed genuine interest in our system but you were not convinced that there were any real economies involved were you to discard your present system in favor of ours.

Although various experiences with other firms who have made the switch gives me complete confidence that you would save a considerable sum,

I understand your reluctance to take the step on nothing more than my say so.

My firm is prepared to put one of our systems engineers in your plant to make a detailed study of the space, payroll and time factors so that you can be given a complete analysis of what the change might accomplish for you. This, of course, will be done at our expense and will create no obligation on your part. We have made such studies before and you can be certain that it will be handled in a manner that will not be disruptive to the personnel involved.

I'll phone you Monday morning to see if we can agree on a mutually convenient time for the study to be made.

Cordially,

SHOCK THEM INTO RECONSIDERATION

Prospects often make wrong decisions. The conscientious, experienced salesman who has taken the trouble to learn about a prospect's circumstances may be sincerely troubled by his inability to make the prospect see his needs as clearly as he should. This is particularly true in the selling of long-term financial plans such as mutual fund investments and life insurance.

Many considerations and new thoughts are brought to the surface in the course of a financial presentation. The variety of subjects discussed may frighten and confuse an unsophisticated prospect. Uncertain prospects will not make affirmative decisions. In many such cases the salesman does well to permit the meeting to end on a negative decision . . . to give the prospect, or prospect and wife . . . time to think.

Under such circumstances a letter designed to jar the prospect into seeing the key issue vividly can be exceptionally effective.

Dear Mr. Newton,

You and Mrs. Newton were extremely gracious last night and I'm grateful. Even though you decided against taking any action, I enjoyed the time we spent together and appreciated your frankness with me.

But I am disturbed.

It is my sincere conviction that you are at the time of life when there is an important need for a sound financial plan to be in effect. I am disturbed because I failed to make all of my thinking clear or failed to demonstrate the graveness of the need.

Even though you said "No" last night, I urge the two of you to continue to discuss the wisdom of taking *some* action as opposed to hoping that the future will take care of itself.

If you'd like to talk with me again, fine, I'd welcome it. But if you decide to work with someone else, that is good too. I'm concerned about you. My making a sale is of minor importance. Good luck and good health to both of you.

Cordially,

————————

Dear Mr. Eagle,

Although we did no business yesterday, I sincerely appreciated the time and attention you gave me. Thank you.

As a businessman you know that selling is a matter of percentages . . . if a salesman calls on enough people, he will make enough sales. Unhappily, your family doesn't enjoy the same advantage. When you refused the family protection plan I offered you yesterday, it was your family that was turned down and they don't have the rule of percentages working for them.

Mr. Eagle, your family needs that extra protection. Your present estate is not enough to enable them to live as you would want them to live if they ever are faced with the need to carry on without you.

Money is deceptive. $20,000 sounds like a lot of money, but if it earned as much as 6% it would provide your family with just about $25 a week. If it is used and not invested, in a few years there won't be anything for them.

Please give your decision a great deal of serious thought, Mr. Eagle. Is it really the right decision?

Sincerely,

In Summary . . . .

When a prospect has heard your presentation and turned you down, a prompt "even though you didn't buy" letter has the power to turn loss into gain. Thoughtfully composed letters of this type can . . .

1. Stamp your name into the prospect's memory so firmly and so favorably that he is likely to call you for some future need or recommend you to others who have current needs for your goods or services.
2. Pave the way for future calls.
3. Enable you to offer something that he *may* want.
4. Jar your prospect into reconsideration of his negative decision.

3

Follow-Up Letters

Sales involving sizeable sums of money seldom are closed at the first attempt. A salesman must follow through. The follow-through effort can be helped substantially by the use of well-planned follow-up letters.

You'll notice two characteristics of the letters in this chapter. One is that they are longer than most. The other is that the majority of them spell out action the salesman will take, as opposed to asking the prospect to take action.

The greatest merit of a brief letter is that it is more likely to be read throughout regardless of the reader's interest or lack of interest. The follow-up letter, however, is addressed to people who have demonstrated some degree of interest in your offer. They are more likely to welcome your letter and read it thoughtfully. But a more compelling reason for the longer letter lies in the basic concept of the follow-up letter. One of the most important functions it serves is to review . . . to summarize . . . to reinforce. Only in unusual cases can this function be handled briefly.

The buyer has not made up his mind. The goal of the follow-up letter, then, is to give him one or more reasons why he should act and act now. Decision-making can be difficult. When you compose a follow-up letter combine persuasion with ease of action. And the easiest way to get action is to take the first physical step yourself. That's why so many of the follow-up letters you are about to read end with the statement that the writer will phone or will come to see the prospect.

YOU HAVE DONE SOMETHING

There are times when you can report that you have done something that will lead to the close of the sale if the prospect doesn't back away.

This is an approach that should be handled with care. Put it to use only when you sincerely believe the action you have taken is in the prospect's best interests or it can cause resentment.

Dear Mr. Allet,

Last week when you and Mrs. Allet came to the showroom you made no secret of your admiration of our stunning new convertibles . . . particularly that blue one with the pale blue leather upholstery.

Spring starts in ten days. There could be no more wonderful time of the year to start enjoying the smooth power and the sheer luxury of your new car.

Right now we have just one blue convertible in stock. I just put a "reserve" on it, because if this is the car of your choice, I wouldn't want you to be disappointed by the delay a factory order involves.

I'll phone tomorrow.

Cordially,

———————

Dear Mrs. Dufour,

To be sure that you wouldn't be disappointed I did something after your visit to our offices several weeks ago.

You expressed particular interest in the Mediterranean cruise on the Galway. That is such a lovely ship and is so much in demand that I took the liberty of putting a temporary reserve on the type of accommodation I knew you would want.

If you decide in the next week or ten days, you can be certain of having one of the most desirable staterooms the Galway offers.

I'll phone in a day or two.

Cordially,

The Motivation of Timeliness

The time factor, where it genuinely exists, is one of your most powerful allies. By all means put it to work in your follow-up letters.

Dear Mr. Breall,

I've asked you to do a very difficult thing.

Breaking a long-time relationship with your current advertising agency can be agonizing. You've developed close relationships with some of the executives and staff members. They've become good friends.

On the other hand, as you expressed it, your advertising has fallen into a well-worn groove. This often happens when an agency has handled one account over a good number of years. I know how excited you are about the fresh thinking we have presented to you. I know that you and I share the conviction that our ideas, once put into action, will have a marked impact on your current acceptance and sales.

You have told me that you'd like to make the change . . . that some day you will. You are approaching the season when budgets and merchandising plans for the coming year must be resolved. This is the time for needed surgery.

I have some thoughts as to how the break may be made without undue distress and I'll be glad to tell you about them. How about lunch next Wednesday? I'll phone that morning to see if you are free.

                                        Cordially,

                        ————————

Dear Mr. Tiller,

If you make the decision to take the space you surveyed in the new Broadview Building, you can add something else to your letterheads . . . prestige.

When your offices are in the most efficient and most modern building in town, people cannot escape the impression that your firm is also efficient and modern.

We have the space and facilities you want and need, Mr. Tiller. By signing your lease now, the area you saw can be finished in accordance with your exact needs.

Construction is nearing completion, and this is the ideal time to make the decision. May I come by with the lease? I'll phone you this week to get your answer.

                                        Cordially,

———————

Dear Mr. Purman,

Mrs. Purman was completely intrigued with the range the two of you looked at a few weeks ago. She fell in love with the ease of cooking it will permit, its capacity and its beauty.

Here's a thought. Mother's Day is coming in just two weeks.

Sincerely,

———————

Dear Mr. and Mrs. Madlow,

Shopping can be terribly confusing.

I know. Last weekend I went with my wife to look for a new spring coat she wanted. By the time we had been to a half dozen stores, we couldn't remember some of the selections we had seen and liked in the first places we visited.

When I had the pleasure of working with you in our showrooms, you were particularly impressed with the dining room group we had assembled in one of our model rooms. It was colonial, and the breakfront had brass insets behind the glass. The table, if you'll recall, extended to the exact length you wanted, and we talked about changing the upholstery on the chairs to harmonize with your drapes.

That set and some of the other pieces you admired are in our warehouse, right here in town. When your new home is ready we can arrange to deliver and install your furniture so that it will be waiting for you when you move in.

If I can help with this or any of your other needs, please call me or drop by.

The greatest happiness to you in your new home. I hope I'll see you in the next few days.

Cordially,

REVIEW THE BENEFITS

Many presentations embrace a number of important sales points. It cannot be assumed that each point will remain clearly in the prospect's mind. Review, therefore, will help the buyer to consolidate his thinking and can lead to a buying decision simply because he is reminded of some of the benefits he will have if he buys.

Dear Mr. Stummer,

With this letter you'll find a copy of a new brochure on the electric typewriter you looked at a few weeks ago.

The brochure has no facts in it that you didn't see for yourself but it is a fine summary of the many economies and advantages it will bring you.

You are a busy man and I realize that the decision on the typewriters is just one of many you must make. Because you are busy, and appreciate the great value of efficiency, I have the conviction that you'll decide that our machines will be the right choice.

I'll phone you in the latter part of this week to ask if you are ready for me to drop by to pick up the order.

Sincerely,

———————

Dear Mr. Imman,

During the weeks that have passed since I had the pleasure of meeting you, I hope you and your associates have found the time to inspect the sample issues of our Weekly Confidential Report.

This I know, because so many business executives have told me so: the Reports bring you information of a type that won't be found in the daily press or trade publications. Our reporters in Washington, for example, are constantly looking for legislative plans in the making. Many issues of the Reports forewarn our readers of things that are being considered. You can see the advantage. Once potentially harmful legislation has been written and introduced, fighting it is an uphill battle. But if you know that such an idea is being considered, the possibility of nipping it in the bud before it takes shape has a much greater chance of succeeding.

The annual fee of $150 is minimal compared with the benefits you may realize by being alerted to coming trends that can help or hurt your business. It is like hiring an expert watchdog for your staff at less than $3 a week.

I'm putting another copy of the enrollment form in with this letter. If you'll hurry it back in the addressed airmail envelope, your service will start next week.

                                                    Sincerely,

Highlight the Prospect's Needs

The review of sales points can be motivating but when your meetings with the prospect have highlighted important needs that demand satisfaction, it pays to concentrate on those needs in your follow-up letter. These, of course, are related to sales points. The difference lies in where you put the emphasis.

Dear Mr. Croydel,

The last time I chatted with you on the phone, you were not fully decided about the investment program I had proposed to you.

Since then, you probably have given it a great deal of study. I've been doing that too. Just this morning I reviewed the details of it and I am more confident than ever that it fits your needs.

These are the main elements that I see:

1. It is a conservative investment that avoids undue risks.

2. Because of the professional management of the portfolio that a mutual fund entails, you don't have to be concerned about your wife having your investment know-how; your estate will consist of your shares plus continuing management and supervision.

3. The program is completely flexible. You can change it in any manner you please at any time.

4. Although the record of performance for the past ten years can't be taken as assurance of what may happen in the future, it does

enable you to judge how well the fund has been able to meet its objectives in the past.

The principal question to ask yourself, Mr. Croydel, is . . . do you know of any other approach to your financial goals that appears more likely to give you what you want?

If your answer to that question is negative, then I think it would be advisable for you to make the decision to start the program now. Time is as important to you as dollars.

I'll phone Monday morning to ask if you are ready to start.

Cordially,

––––––––––

Dear Mr. Farming,

You assured me that you would be giving a lot of thought to increasing your life insurance protection, and I'm sure you have.

In my opinion there is one key consideration.

You have carried the same amount of coverage for the past eleven years. You are still a young man with a young family. In eleven years you have seen the prices you pay for everything increase considerably. Eleven years ago you decided how much money your family would need were you not part of the picture. Unquestionably, they would need more today. On top of that you have made fine progress and your standard of living has risen. This, in itself, dictates the need for broader protection. You would not want your family to move down the living scale.

Looking ahead, more inflation is in sight and you most certainly anticipate continuing your personal climb up the economic ladder.

Now, before your insurance age and the cost of insurance increases, is the logical time to make your insurance program more realistic.

These, as I see it, are the compelling reasons why you should act at once. The only negative I can see is the natural reluctance we all have to spend money. This isn't spending, Mr. Farming. It is sending money ahead for the benefit of your family and for the building of cash values for yourself.

When you consider those facts, don't you believe that you should start now with the revised program? I will call you later in the week.

Sincerely,

Reveal Hidden Values

Many products and services permit the salesman to show his prospects that, in addition to the apparent values and benefits, there are other values that are less obvious. Dramatizing the presence of hidden values is akin to offering something extra. The skillful use of a hidden value in what you sell can be the deciding factor when the prospect is undecided.

Dear Mr. Overton,

There's one thing missing from the survey I gave you on your current shipping costs and service as opposed to the costs and services you'd enjoy if you adopted air freight.

While the facts and figures are as complete and as accurate as we could make them, they do not reveal some other factors that may have even greater importance. They don't, for example, show the immense satisfaction of your customers who will get their shipments with unusual speed and reliability. Nor do they show the increased enthusiasm of your salesmen who will have a powerful extra selling point and additional confidence in their company's progressive management.

How soon can we start?

Cordially,

———————

Dear Mr. Cannin,

This morning I took from the files a carbon of our estimate to completely air condition your home. After reviewing it, I'm completely satisfied that our engineer did his customary careful survey and has recommended a system that is ideal for your needs. I am equally satisfied that, from your viewpoint, the price is a good one.

But there are some things that the estimate does not show.

For one thing, it doesn't show the continuing interest we take in every installation. You called us in because your neighbor recommended us. That is how our business has been built. We dedicate ourselves to making every customer an enthusiastic booster of our services.

Another thing the estimate can't reveal is the solid pleasure and the good health that are part and parcel of well planned, smoothly functioning air conditioning.

Your parents and mine lived without the blessings of air conditioned comfort and managed very well. That, however, was before the days of working and shopping in air cooled areas. We are conditioned to scientifically cooled air today and the contrast when we come home, if air conditioning is absent, is unpleasant and can be unhealthy.

Hot weather days will be with us soon. Our installation department is getting busier with each passing day. My sincere recommendation is that you give us the word to start now so that your home will be a haven of pleasant comfort throughout the summer.

I'll phone in the next day or two.

Cordially,

Answer the Objection

One of the principal advantages you have when writing a follow-up letter is that you have met and talked with the prospect. You know a good deal about his thinking and his attitudes and you usually know if there is one major objection. Concentrate on the objection. Think of the most effective answer you can offer and make your answer the theme of your letter.

Dear Mr. Jacks,

From the various ideas we have exchanged at our meetings I am convinced of two things.

Number one, there is no question but that the use of our computer service would afford you inventory controls and a billing procedure that will add immeasurably to the efficiency of your operation; will add to the reliability of your controls; will speed your cash flow and reduce administrative costs.

Number two, your reason for not making the move at this time is based on your lack of conviction that the conversion can be made without confusion and error.

You are right to have such misgivings.

Computers perform with extraordinary accuracy and speed, but the programming and the input of data are subject to human error.

But, Mr. Jacks, your mind can be at ease.

Our plan calls for weeks of parallel operation with your current methods before switching over. Day after day you and our specialists will be comparing the output of your current system and that of the computer. Your present system will not be put aside until you are 100% satisfied that our programming is precise and that the input is thoroughly accurate.

Furthermore, Mr. Jacks, until you and our people are satisfied there will be no billing for our services. The price quoted to you for the programming and preparation of the input data includes the testing, or de-bugging, period. It is we who accept the risk of encountering time consuming problems.

Consider the advantages you will enjoy, devoid of risk on your part. The sooner you tell us to start, the sooner the rewards will be available to you.

I'll be in touch with you next week with the hope that we can put our programmers to work for you.

Cordially,

BE IMAGINATIVE

The exercise of imagination has exceptional power to close sales. Concentrate on the prospect's viewpoint . . . his problems. With his viewpoint firmly in mind, against the background of your extensive knowledge of what you are selling, try to arrive at a suggestion you can make or an action you can take that will have pronounced effect on his thinking. Be colorful. Be exciting. Use an imaginative idea that demonstrates your understanding of the prospect's basic needs and interests. Use an imaginative idea that he will enjoy accepting or anticipating.

Dear Mr. Maggon,

We're ready to go.

Following the interesting discussion we had about your weekly publication, I had a meeting with members of our staff and we worked out a detailed program for the handling of your newsletter. I wanted to be absolutely certain that we'd be fully prepared to deliver the promises I made. I am certain.

You outlined to me the problems you have had with your present supplier, and I am fully confident that those problems would not arise in our shop. Our Friday night and all-day Saturday shifts can produce, address and mail your publication with efficiency and reliability.

Admittedly, you'll be paying slightly more, but the fact that your subscribers will receive every issue of your newsletter on time means a higher renewal rate. This will more than offset the difference.

We're ready to go, Mr. Maggon. I will phone Monday at ten to ask if you are ready to go with us.

Cordially,

———————

Dear Mr. Lighter,

You and I have had a number of stimulating and enjoyable conversations. But, Mr. Lighter, conversations don't ring the bell on your cash register or add profits to your statement.

Hundreds of good merchants carry our line and have improved their businesses because they do. The best testimony to that is their constant reorders.

Next Thursday afternoon I'm going to walk into your office with just two things . . . a smile and an order book. I won't say a word. I'll just put my order book on your desk and sit back while you write your requirements for your starting inventory.

You can make money with our line and this is the way to start.

Cordially,

———————

Dear Mr. Henrich,

Since you were here and reviewed the fine convention facilities our hotel offers, you have seen your alternate choices. Now it is a question of making the final decision.

I have a suggestion.

From your experience in handling your Association's annual conventions over the years, undoubtedly, you have observed that the most successful ones were in those hotels where service was outstandingly good. But this is something you usually can't measure until after the fact.

I know how good our service is but, at present, you don't.

With this letter I am enclosing a card with the names and phone numbers of the heads of three Associations who held their conventions in our hotel during the past six months. Each of them is so enthused about the service and the treatment their members enjoyed that they have agreed to accept your collect phone calls. I may be biased, but they are not.

Please phone them and I'll phone you next week.

Cordially,

In Summary . . . .

Your follow-up letters can help your prospects to make affirmative decisions if you . . .

1. Show that you have done something for their benefit.
2. Capitalize on a genuine time factor.
3. Remind them of the key selling points.
4. Emphasize their needs.
5. Bring out hidden values.
6. Provide sound answers to their objections.
7. Use an imaginative idea.

4

Letters Following a Presentation

You were given the opportunity to make a presentation. A decision is in abeyance and you plan to see the prospect again.

You have sound reasons to feel a genuine sense of appreciation for the opportunity you have been given...for the time your prospect took to hear your story. If you express your appreciation with a letter mailed the day after the presentation, you will improve your chances of making the sale.

Dear Mr. Kelly,

I thoroughly enjoyed meeting you yesterday.

My sincerest hope is that you found that the time you took to meet with me proved to be rewarding. Between now and our next meeting I will be doing a good deal of thinking about the questions we discussed for I have the conviction that there are a number of things I can do that may prove valuable to you.

The notation has been made on my calendar that I'm to have the pleasure of seeing you again at 10:30 next Tuesday morning, and I look forward to that.

Cordially,

31

If your first meeting closed on a vague note, with no firm appointment for a subsequent meeting...

Dear Mr. Allen,

Many thanks for taking time out of your busy day to see me yesterday. I thoroughly enjoyed meeting you and found it a stimulating, challenging experience.

We gave each other a number of things to think about and I look forward to exchanging ideas with you when we get together again. I'll phone you in the next day or two to arrange an appointment that will be convenient for you.

Cordially,

————————

Dear Mr. Anderson,

It was good of you to give me the opportunity to present my ideas to you yesterday. Meeting you was a genuine pleasure for me, and I look forward to seeing you again.

You wanted more time to think about my suggestions, and I hope that the things I told you and the material I left with you have given you reason to believe that it will pay you to explore these thoughts further.

I plan to phone you Tuesday morning to ask when it will be convenient for us to meet again.

Cordially,

Something More to Offer

On many occasions a first meeting will uncover some facts that will result in your gathering some figures, literature, designs or ideas to handle problems or questions that the prospect raised.

Dear Mr. Minter,

I've been working.

Since our recent meeting, which I enjoyed so much, I have been doing a good deal of thinking about some of the thoughtful questions you raised. As a result I have gathered together some materials that you are going to find unusually interesting. I look forward to the opportunity of presenting them to you.

If you'll be good enough to tell your secretary when you can see me for another fifteen-minute session, I'll call her Monday morning and will adjust my schedule to fit yours.

Cordially,

If the facts or materials you prepare, following the first meeting, are items the prospect asked you to get . . .

Dear Mr. Kew,

I have the information you want.

As soon as I left your office yesterday, I hurried back to our plant and got together with our chief engineer to review your needs with him. I think you'll be as thoroughly delighted with the solution he proposed as I am. Now I know how he became chief engineer.

Will you have time to see me at three o'clock Monday afternoon so that I can show you his ideas? I will phone you Monday morning to learn if you can make it at that time.

Please accept my sincerest thanks for your interest and your courtesy. I hope that this marks the start of a long and very pleasant relationship. I think it will become just that.

Cordially,

The enthusiasm and the optimism displayed in that letter are bound to be contagious. The prospect will be eager to see the idea that was created to fit his needs.

Dear Mr. Burns,

When I left you yesterday, I went to see our sales manager and told him of your comments on our quantity discounts.

I'm happy to tell you that he was most cooperative and I am confident, now, that you'll be happy with the terms.

May I see you at eleven on Monday morning? I'll phone on Friday to see if you'll be able to make a date at that time.

My sincerest thanks.

Cordially,

———————

Dear Mr. Palmer,

I burned the midnight oil last night.

When we were together in your office, you raised a point that gave me considerable food for thought. I now have completed a statistical analysis, covering the past ten years, that shows the outcome of your present use of pension funds and what the results would have been had those same dollars been employed, over the same period of time, in the manner I have suggested to you.

To play safe I am having my figures checked by our accountants this morning. As soon as I have their verification, I'll drop by your office with the work sheets and the results so that you can see the full comparison.

I thoroughly enjoyed meeting you yesterday and look forward to having that pleasure repeated.

Cordially,

There is one important element in each of the three preceding letters. Each one of them paints a picture of activity on behalf of the prospect. The reader knows that the salesman, and others, have been investing time, thought and effort for his potential benefit. A sense of obligation is added to curiosity and the possibility of gain. The likelihood of agreement to a second meeting is greatly enhanced.

REMINDERS OF BENEFITS

In the course of any sales presentations a skilled salesman features certain key selling points and quickly becomes aware of the one or ones that appear to be most important to the prospect. The reminder of the point or points that had the strongest appeal can be used effectively in the "thanks for listening" letter.

Dear Mr. North,

Meeting you yesterday was a great pleasure for me. Thank you for making it possible.

After leaving you I did a good deal of thinking about the points we had discussed. You displayed particular interest in the Early American fixtures you saw in our catalogue. I can clearly picture that installation. They would not only add to the attractiveness of your store, but your employees would find them so much easier to work with and the atmosphere so pleasant that I am convinced that the problem of employee turnover, which concerns you, would be reduced a significant degree.

I have sent for some enlarged color photos of the fixtures. The moment they arrive I'll hurry them to you.

Cordially,

————

Dear Mr. Graham,

It always has been my contention that the most rewarding part of my work is the people I meet. You underscored that benefit yesterday. Thank you for receiving me so graciously.

One of the things I particularly appreciated was your alert understanding of the exceptional benefits in the policy we discussed, particularly the guaranteed return of all premiums in addition to the face amount. Many people, I've observed, are more concerned with what they pay as opposed to the far greater consideration . . . what they are providing for their loved ones.

I'm enclosing a quick digest of all the benefits and the features of the policy for your review. If you are free for lunch one day next week, I'd be grateful for the opportunity to see you again and to answer any questions that you may want to ask.

I'll phone Monday to make the arrangements.

Cordially,

―――――――

Dear Mr. Custer,

My warmest thanks for seeing me yesterday.

You are a busy man but you took the time to permit me to show how my firm might be of substantial assistance to your company.

This letter is an attempt to partially repay the favor.

In the course of my discussion with you, I covered a series of reasons why it might be to your company's best interests to accept the proposition I offered. I am well aware of the fact that there were more points made than I could expect you to recall in detail. For your convenience, therefore, I am enclosing a check list of those points. There is room under each for you to note any questions you may have . . . or to check if you would like more details.

When I have the pleasure of seeing you again, I think you'll find the list and your notations an effective means of saving your time.

I look forward to the pleasure of seeing you again and will phone in a few days for the appointment.

Cordially,

Using What You Have Learned

Every meeting with a prospect provides a means of learning many things. Some of the things you will learn will be about the prospect's business or personal circumstances and some will constitute random information about him as a person. In your "thanks for listening" letter any evidence you can give of your interest in the prospect as a person, or his business problems . . . particularly if they are unrelated to your own interests . . . will be appreciated.

Dear Mr. Winter,

I just wanted you to know how much I enjoyed meeting you yesterday.

While we were together you mentioned the trouble you were having finding some sound statistics on that new territory you are planning to open. I did some checking and I learned that there is a report available from the Census Bureau in Washington, D. C. that may contain a good deal of the information you'd like to have. I took the liberty of sending for a copy and as soon as it arrives I'll bring it by.

Thank you for telling me that you will study the proposal I left with you. If you have any questions regarding any part of it, please phone me. I'll be happy to give you the answers.

Cordially,

––––––––––

Dear Mr. Apple,

Talking with you and Mrs. Apple about starting a college education fund for Harold, Jr. was a stimulating experience for me. Thank you for inviting me into your lovely home and for your interest and courtesy.

In the course of our discussion you said that you'd like to see your son go to Harvard. Even though it will be a number of years before he is ready to apply, experience has shown me that it pays to know a college's entrance requirements long in advance. Knowing them enables you to guide your boy in the selection of elective subjects and, in some cases, what types of extracurricular activities might be important to him.

With that in mind I wrote to Harvard's Admissions Officer and asked him to send you their catalogue. You should have it soon.

I'm looking forward to seeing you and Mrs. Apple next Wednesday and hope that we can launch that college plan at that time. I know how gratifying it will be to both of you to know that you aren't leaving the big financing problem to chance.

Cordially,

––––––––––

Dear Mr. Free,

Thank you. I deeply appreciate the time you took yesterday to listen to my proposal.

When I admired that picture on your desk of that husky eight-year-old son of yours, you told me of his great interest in baseball. I happened to come across the enclosed baseball schedule for the coming season and I thought you'd enjoy taking it home to him.

I look forward to our meeting next week.

Cordially,

BEING SLIGHTLY UNCONVENTIONAL

Salesmen are, to a great extent, experts in showmanship. It is not at all inappropriate, therefore, to use a degree of showmanship in your letter writing. The unusual attracts extra attention and is remembered longer.

The style of your letter should be in tune with you and your own personality. But the personality and the characteristics of your prospect must also be given consideration. If your prospect is a highly conventional person, avoid the use of an unconventional letter. But if he is a colorful, imaginative person, there is no need to hesitate about a letter with "a difference."

You're great, Mr. Solo . . .

You are. Busy as you are, you pulled out all stops for me. You stopped your phone from ringing. You stopped your door from swinging. You gave me the extreme courtesy of undivided attention and interest.

And I'm pulling out all stops for you.

During the next five days, before we meet again, I'll be digging into the thoughtful questions you raised. When we get together next Thursday I'll be loaded with answers and materials to back them up.

Many thanks . . .

————————

I'm grateful, Mr. Pine . . .

Yesterday you gave me the priceless gift of your time and attention.

I'm greatly encouraged by your interest and devoutly hope that the idea seed I planted with you will grow and flourish . . . I have the feeling that it will.

Your phone will ring Tuesday around ten. I'll be on the other end asking when we can have our next session together.

My heartiest thanks . . .

People You Have Known

All of the "thanks for listening" letters preceding have been addressed to new prospects . . . people you never met prior to the presentations referred to. But you also make presentations to established customers or to non-customers you have called on before or know socially.

Most of the previous letters easily can be adapted for use with those you know, but there are cases where letters of a different type are required.

Dear Mr. Pell,

It was so good to see you again yesterday. Thanks for finding the time for my visit.

You assured me that you would give serious consideration to the proposal I made, and I know you will. When you are ready to discuss it further, just give me a ring and I'll come running.

Cordially,

————————

Dear Pete,

I don't have to tell you how eagerly I look forward to your decision. Grand seeing you again. Thanks for the fruitful session we had.

I'll give you a ring the later part of next week to check. In the meantime, if I can help you with any facts, figures, questions or anything else, just pick up the phone and tell me what I can do. I'll do it.

My best, Pete . . .

———————

Dear Mr. Miller,

Over the years I've always enjoyed doing business with you and I come away from each meeting with you feeling an inch or two taller.

I appreciate the consideration you are giving to our newest proposition.

As we agreed, I'll pick you up at your office at noon on Wednesday for lunch and look forward to that. I'm confident that you know from the dealings you've had with my firm, that you can put your full reliance in the manner in which we'll follow through if you give me the go-ahead when we meet.

Cordially,

In Summary . . . .

When a new prospect or an old customer gives you the opportunity to make a presentation, and a decision is to be made at a later date, you can increase the possibilities of winning the order with a "thanks for listening" letter.

The basic elements of a "thanks for listening" letter are a showing of sincere appreciation and interest in the reader. In addition to the basic elements, these additional factors will add to the power of your letters:

1. Pinpointing the day and time of the next meeting or detailing the action you will take to arrange a second meeting.
2. Offering to bring additional related facts, figures or materials.
3. Displaying enthusiasm and optimism about the likelihood of acceptance.
4. Providing answers to questions raised at the first meeting.
5. Demonstrating the degree of your interest by describing actions being taken in his behalf.

6. Reminding him of key sales points, particularly those that interest him the most.
7. Evidence of thoughtful things you have done or are doing that are unrelated to what you sell.
8. Employing showmanship in your letters if it is in keeping with your personality and the personality of the recipient.
9. Giving full recognition to old relationships where they exist.

5

Letters of Invitation to Visit Store, Office or Exhibit

While the problem of increasing store traffic generally is handled by management, salesmen can develop their own clientele and increase their commission income by using the mails. A retail salesman knows the people who have dealt with him in the past . . . he knows something about their likes and dislikes and he knows their names and addresses. Regular customers can be made more regular if the salesman uses his knowledge.

When a new shipment of men's suits comes to a clothing store, for example, an alert salesman examining the fresh shipment readily can bring to mind the names of customers who would be particularly attracted to the new merchandise.

Dear Mr. Emerson,

I don't know who he is and I don't think you do either. But there's a man in California who must know you.

Yesterday afternoon we received our first shipment of the new line of summer suits designed and tailored by our favorite California source. As soon as I saw them, I thought of you. They are exactly the types of suits you like so well. They are high style . . . outstandingly different without being at all freakish. The fabrics and colors are beautiful, too.

I just hope that you can find the time to drop in this week while the full assortment is here. I think you'll agree that the man who designed them must have had you in mind.

Cordially,

Creative imagination can be used with great effect in luring old or new customers to a store.

Dear Mr. Rose,

Could you and Mrs. Rose arrange to be here at 8 o'clock Wednesday evening?

On that day, at that hour, there will be a color telecast of a tour of Italy's finest art galleries. From what I've heard, it will be one of the most beautiful and inspiring programs ever.

Not only would I like you to enjoy this show, but I can think of no better way of demonstrating to you the current perfection of color television. You'll be thrilled with it and you'll see what a new world of pleasure ownership of a color set can bring into your home.

I do hope you can make it and look forward to seeing you.

Cordially,

In the letter to Mr. Rose the invitation was based on a specific program. This is an added inducement, indeed, but the concept can be employed regardless of special programs. The heart of the idea is to think in terms of what will be most appealing to potential customers, as opposed to thinking exclusively about the selling points in the merchandise to be offered. The invitation to see a good show in color is far more likely to entice than a recitation of selling points about the set.

There are countless ways to make effective use of your sense or knowledge of a prospect's viewpoint. A furniture salesman may come to the conclusion that a good market to tackle might be the refurnishing of doctors' reception rooms. But first he must face the problem of how he can motivate doctors to *want* to redecorate. If he finds the answer to that problem and uses it as the foundation of his letter, he will enjoy considerably more success than he would were he to simply use his letters to tell doctors to visit him when they were ready to refurnish.

Dear Dr. Jordan,

Have you ever listened to your reception room?

I don't refer to the coversations of patients . . . I am talking about what your furniture is saying. The way a doctor's reception room is furnished says a lot to the people who come there.

Maybe your reception room says fine things. But if you suspect that it does not, please accept this warm invitation to visit with me at our showrooms. You will see a variety of reception room treatments that speak of their owners in very flattering terms. And speaking of terms . . . the cost of redoing your reception room can be quite reasonable.

I hope I'll have the pleasure of seeing you.

Cordially,

The furniture salesman can also find excellent prospects by watching the newspapers. Reports of people buying or building new homes certainly pinpoint prospects who have reasons to be interested in hearing from and calling on you.

Dear Mr. Newhouse,

Congratulations on the home you are building.

We've done some building too. We have built a reputation for having the smartest, best constructed furniture available . . . for having exceptionally talented interior decorators . . . for being delightfully cooperative with our customers . . . for being happily reasonable in both prices and payment terms.

Please come in. It would be my great pleasure to work with you and Mrs. Newhouse in planning the furnishing of your new home.

Cordially,

Various seasons of the year should inspire the use of letters written and mailed by salesmen. Christmas is a prime example.

Dear Mr. Dally,

Christmas isn't too far off and I'd love to help you to select a lovely gift of furs for Mrs. Dally. At this time of the year our selections are at their peak. You'll see some exciting things at almost any price range you desire.

Won't you come in? It will be nice to see you again.

Cordially,

THE BENEFITS OF BREVITY

Letters of invitation often give you the welcome opportunity to use extremely brief letters. If there is no need to go into a great deal of explanation or special pleading, by all means avoid them.

Brief letters not only assure more readership but they are considerably easier to produce.

One of the most effective letters of invitation that ever came my way was written by a fishing captain I had gone out with on several occasions. This was what he sent me...

Dear Mr. Nauheim,

They're running.

Capt. Bill

Two words is something of a record for a letter with a powerful sales message, but you can be mighty brief in many instances.

Dear Mrs. Shelby,

Have you been reading and hearing about the exciting new spring suits and coats Paris has introduced?

We've got them!

Cordially,

———————

Dear Mrs. Collins,

If you've been told that color television sets are in short supply . . . that it is difficult to find the model you want . . . it's true.

But not here.

Sincerely,

———————

Dear Mr. Shrader,

The new models are here. They're fabulously beautiful to look at and to drive.

Come in and drive one. You'll be thrilled.

Cordially,

———————

Dear Mr. Paton,

We have a sale only once a year. But when we do the savings are substantial.

The sale starts Monday and ends Saturday.

Sincerely,

SUBSTANTIAL LETTERS FOR SUBSTANTIAL SALES

The appeal of short letters is undeniable but most people make the error of overestimating the importance of keeping business letters brief. The length of a letter is not the factor that makes it win or lose. If the *facts* in a letter require many words, and the words are interesting and appealing, it doesn't matter how long a letter is.

The letters that follow are not unusually long, but will appear long in contrast with the very brief ones you have just read. The statements about long letters have been included here as an antidote to exhibiting short ones. I want to play no part in perpetuating the fiction that business letters always must be brief.

An officer of a bank frequently plays the part of a salesman. He is interested in attracting new customers to his bank.

Dear Mr. Montcalm,

Please accept this invitation to use something we have.

We are a very competitive bank, and that isn't easy. Banking services are quite uniform and so are interest rates. Our competitiveness shows in the attitudes we take in dealing with our customers. We take a deeply sincere interest in them.

This goes well beyond greeting them by name when they come in. There are many things a bank can do for its customers and some of them are almost unknown. By learning all we can about the people who deal with us, we are able to bring some of these little-known services to their attention.

For example, I was chatting with one customer recently and he happened to mention his concern about a fairly substantial sale he was expecting to close the following day. He hadn't been able to get enough information about the buyer to feel certain about the credit to be extended. An important part of our business is to have extensive sources of credit information. Within a few hours we had detailed information for him that put his mind at ease.

If you will consider using us as your bank, I'll be most grateful if you'll make a point of dropping in and asking for me. I'd like to meet you . . . to get to know you . . . to learn something about your activities so that I'll be in a position to be as helpful to you as I'd like to be.

Sincerely,

In recent years banks, for the most part, have worked hard to overcome their traditional image as cold, stuffy institutions. Letters written in a warmly human manner can help in that worthy effort.

Investment firms face the same problem.

Dear Mr. Lemmer,

Do you ever do any investing?

If you do, I would certainly enjoy working with you. My firm has splendid facilities for research and for the handling of orders. It would be my great pleasure to learn what your investment aims and ideas are and to give you the benefit of our ideas.

The next time you are in our neighborhood please drop in and ask for me.

Cordially,

The real estate salesman, when dealing in homes, has the great advantage of appealing to some very strong emotional feelings. It is only an advantage, however, if he recognizes the opportunities it represents and makes fullest use of them.

Dear Mr. Gilmour,

I'd like to paint a picture for you and Mrs. Gilmour.

It's a verbal picture . . .

> Next summer, when you finish work Friday afternoon you'll pick your wife up at the house and drive just 37 miles out Route 89 to Lake Mirror and park your car in the breezeway of your own lakeside cottage.

> Your cottage has two bedrooms, a big roomy living room with a picture window facing the lake, a powder room in addition to a full bath and a completely modern kitchen with a cute little dining nook.

> You've got your own dock for swimming and boating, or just for sitting and fishing.

Do you like the picture?

Let's develop it and enlarge it.

Take that drive on Route 89 this weekend. I'll be there in the sales office. Let me show you that picture in reality. I'm particularly looking forward to watching the look of delighted surprise on your faces when I tell you the price and terms.

See you this weekend.

Cordially,

INVITATION TO TRADE SHOWS AND FAIRS

Participation in a trade show or fair generally represents a considerable investment of time and dollars. The salesman who will be on duty at the booth can capitalize on the situation by increasing his opportunities to draw good prospects through friendly letters.

Dear Mr. Trammer,

You'll enjoy using the enclosed tickets.

The tickets will admit you to the Business Equipment Show on Monday, Tuesday or Wednesday of next week, at the Grand Hotel.

My company's booth is number 27 and I'll be there with a gift for you. So be sure to look me up.

Hundreds of office machines, devices and supplies will be on display and some of the demonstrations will be fascinating. You'll see a number of new products being introduced.

I'm sure you'll find that the time you spend at the show will be profitable. With such a variety of new methods and products to be seen, there are bound to be a few that will have particular interest and value for you.

I'll be looking for you at booth 27.

Cordially,

———————————

Dear Mrs. Paulson,

Please be my guest at the Home Decorating Show next week.

I warn you, though, you'll come away from it with your head spinning. You'll see so many fascinating new ideas in home decoration you'll be full of plans for your own home.

While you are there, come and relax with me. I'm planning on having a number of comfortable chairs at my booth where the ladies I invite can sit and give their feet a well-earned rest. There will be coffee and Cokes there too.

And just between us, I believe that you'll find some of the most intriguing new ideas in my booth. Come see. The enclosed ticket has all the details about when and where.

Cordially,

In Summary . . . .

"Come see me" letters must be written from the prospect's viewpoint. Letters of invitation will succeed if you give the readers sufficient reasons why they may gain something by accepting.

To find and use sound "reasons why" people should come to see you . . .

1. If writing to old customers, trade on what you know about each one.
2. Apply creative imagination to your invitation.
3. Dramatize the motivations that may induce prospects to call.
4. Search the newspapers for people who have reasons to see you.
5. Use the timeliness of seasons, holidays, news events to fortify the reasons you offer.
6. If you can highlight a strong reason why with just a sentence or two, by all means do so.
7. The sincere showing of human warmth and interest can serve as strong reasons why people should come to see you.

May I come to see you? ...

On pages 56 through 61 of this
chapter is one of the bonus features of this book . . . *a proven
Appointment-Winning System.*

6

Letters Asking
for Appointments

Few things will warm a salesman's heart and fatten his wallet more
than the opportunity to meet with a good prospect under favorable
circumstances.

A thoughtfully written letter can be the key that opens the doors to an
endless flow of prospects.

Appointment-seeking letters will take many forms. What form a letter
should take depends on a variety of factors ... *what you sell ... how
you'll follow through ... previous contacts ... how you found the prospect* ... and more.

WHAT YOU SELL

Tangible products. There will be great differences between the letter
approach you will make if you want an appointment to present a popu-
lar, well-known, heavily advertised product as opposed to a product or
service that the prospect knows nothing about.

The well-known product appointment request can be handled with
just a brief letter ...

Dear Mr. Blue,

You've been hearing and reading about the X-ELL Office Copier. Now you can see it and try it yourself right on your own desk. Once you have seen the brilliant sharpness of the copies it makes . . . the speed and ease with which any quantity of clean, dry copies can be produced . . . and I tell you how economical the machine and the copies are . . . I'll probably have more trouble taking it away from you than making a sale. And I promise that I won't try to take it away.

The card I've enclosed with this letter has your name and address on it. It's addressed to me and needs no postage. Just drop the card in the mail and I'll drop in at your office for the demonstration.

I look forward to meeting you.

Cordially,

The letter does a number of things. Instantly, the reader knows what you offer. With almost equal speed he learns that he'll be given the opportunity to see, test, play with the machine himself. The selling points are presented with clarity and brevity. There is a light touch of humor that is calculated to make him feel that the salesman is a pleasant person. The letter closes with an action request that stresses the ease of compliance.

Summed up, if the prospect has any possible interest in the machine, this brisk and pleasant invitation is hard to resist.

The unknown or little known item may call for extra effort.

Dear Mr. Brown,

I'd like to make an exchange with you. For 12 minutes of your time I'll give you 208 extra hours this year.

That sounds exaggerated, but I think it is true.

My firm has spent many years developing a new, dry, high-speed office copier. Test after test, under customer use, has shown that the average time an executive saved by putting the machine on his desk is 4 hours a week . . . 208 hours a year.

When I come to see you, I won't have much to say. Our machine, the E-Z Office Copier, will do most of the talking. All I ask is the opportunity to put it on your desk, give you one brief demonstration, and then let you use it youself so that you can fully appreciate the ease and speed of operation . . . the quality of the sharp, clean, dry copies it produces.

For myself, I'll reserve the pleasure of telling you how low the cost is.

The card I've enclosed with this letter has your name and address on it. It's addressed to me and needs no postage. Just drop the card in the mail and I'll drop in at your office for the demonstration.

Cordially,

While the letter to Mr. Brown is not much longer than the one to Mr. Blue, it uses some extra sales points in the effort to overcome the handicap of offering an unknown product. One vital element is the opening sentence. You are approaching Mr. Brown as an utter stranger and, the chances are, he is a busy man. He is also a normal human being who shies away from the unfamiliar. The letter's opening hits hard to arouse his curiosity to the extent that he is almost certain to read what follows.

Intangibles. When an intangible service is offered, the approach calls for other considerations. Demonstrations or pictures of something that can be touched, seen, tasted and tried are dramatic lures that can't be used. Your approach has to be even more imaginative since you must stir the imagination of the prospect.

Dear Mr. Cerise,

My career is dedicated to shocking people.

There are two things I've observed. One is that the Research Division of the Social Security Board has learned that 70% of family heads over the age of 65 have less than $2,000 when they retire. That certainly is shocking. The second observation is that most people are deeply involved in the daily business of making enough income to handle today's high prices and high taxes. They seldom take time out to look ahead and to make plans that may spare them from being part of that shockingly large group.

To hear my ideas and suggestions will cost you nothing and will create no obligation. I'm confident that you will find that our meeting will give you some useful ideas whether or not you adopt any specific proposals I may make.

Please tell me on the enclosed, addressed and postage paid card, when and where we can get together.

Sincerely,

If the letter succeeds in making the reader thoughtful and somewhat uncomfortable about his own situation, it has a good chance of winning the appointment. If the shoe fits, the reader can put it on, but the letter studiously avoids any direct finger pointing. It speaks of the failure of "people" to plan. The reader is not accused directly. Even the "people" are excused for their carelessness so that the reader, should he feel that he is one of the guilty, will not feel embarrassed should he meet the salesman.

In the request for action the prospect is given ample assurance that he is promising nothing more than his ears and an open mind but he is shown that there can be benefits even if he does not buy.

How You'll Follow Through

All advertising ... and letters asking for appointments constitute one form of advertising ... must be planned with the next step in mind if you receive no reply. The decision can be to take *no* next step. In most cases it pays to follow through. The follow-through may consist of further letters, a phone call or a physical call. The physical call is the least desirable. The main reason for using letters seeking appointments is to eliminate poor prospects and to find good ones ... to fill your working hours with firm dates with logical prospects who know what you sell and have enough interest to invite you to tell your story.

Follow-up letters. If you choose your prospect list with thoughtful care there is no reason to discard the names of those who failed to take the action you asked for in your first letter. You have no way of knowing why there was no response. The prospect may have been away on a trip or absent because of illness. The letter may have reached him when he was exceptionally busy and preoccupied. You may have reached him when he was in a poor, pessimistic frame of mind.

If you employ a series of letters the likelihood is that, sooner or later, one will arrive at just the right moment and he'll act.

A second attribute of a series of letters is that each can stress a different sales point or appeal. One may be the exactly right appeal from the prospect's viewpoint.

And if your company, product or service is unknown or almost so, each succeeding letter will serve to establish your firm and your offer in the reader's mind until he begins to feel a degree of familiarity with them. The guard against the unknown will begin to drop.

Follow-up letters should avoid the space-wasting effort of reminding the reader of previous letters. If he remembers them, he doesn't need to be reminded. If he does not remember them, your references to them won't help and there is always the danger that such reminders may be taken as scolding.

You wrote one letter to Mr. Blue about your well-advertised office copier. The first follow-up letter takes a fresh approach.

Dear Mr. Blue,

About three o'clock yesterday I was in the office of a busy lawyer who has an X-ELL Office Copier on his desk. The copier takes up less space than a typewriter. While I was with him he took a phone call from a client and covered a page of a large pad with notes. He still was talking when he ran those notes through his desk copier. By the time he had hung up, the original was on his desk for action and the copy was in his basket for filing.

Although I've seen and heard of scores of uses for the X-ELL desk model, undoubtedly, there are as many more I haven't run into yet. You probably will find some uses I've never imagined.

Nothing I'd enjoy more than meeting you and letting you experiment with the X-ELL yourself.

Mailing the card I've put with this letter will bring me running. Phoning me at 365-6886 will bring me that much sooner.

Cordially,

There's a stimulating challenge in this narrative-type letter. The prospect is encouraged to picture himself finding new uses for the machine ...new efficiencies for himself. This letter plays more on his emotions than the original letter, which was an appeal to logic. Thus, the salesman who mails a series of letters to well-chosen prospects is able to play one card at a time in his search for the winner.

The salesman who wrote Mr. Cerise and tried to shock him into an appointment has a vast number of other appeals at his disposal. If the shock approach didn't bring a reply, he might resort to a totally different appeal.

> **Dear Mr. Cerise,**
>
> **No one ever spends money through me.**
>
> **That's a peculiar statement from a salesman but it happens to be true.**
>
> **My role is to help people to review their financial situations and their future needs. If, through my years of training and experience in helping many clients, I see opportunities for financial improvement, I point them out. If they accept my suggestions, they don't spend money; they transfer money from one place to another . . . but only if they are convinced that they may be better off by doing so.**
>
> **Whether or not I can prove helpful to you remains to be seen. Perhaps you'll agree though that you owe yourself the opportunity to find out. There's no fee for counselling and you are under no obligation to accept any ideas I may propose.**
>
> **Please use the enclosed card to let me know when we can meet.**
>
> > **Sincerely,**

No shocks this time, but this letter is calculated to make Mr. Cerise feel that he may be missing something of real importance if he fails to act...that he has little or nothing to lose if he meets the writer...that he may have something to gain.

A Proven Appointment-Winning System

Nothing in the process of making appointments has proven to be more reliable than a combination of a letter and a telephone call. Any salesman who devotes his time to outside calls on an appointment basis can adopt the combination as the certain means of filling his days with good appointments. It never wears out.

Nothing in life is perfect but be careful, slow and deliberate if you depart from any of the detailed elements of the description to follow. This method has been experimented with and thoroughly tested in many hundreds of sales offices and by many thousands of salesmen in a broad variety of businesses. In almost every case where it did not show anticipated results, investigation disclosed that there had been a change made. Even a slight variation may be destructive.

In most fields this program has produced 3 appointments for every 10 people approached.

Such results don't happen the first day the method is used. They come with practice, patience and the growth of self-confidence.

Here is the program:

1. *The list.* The preparation of the list of prospects, in any appointment-seeking programs, calls for thoughtful care. Aim high. Choose prospects with real buying potential. Don't, however, be unrealistic. Since you are going to contact the people on your list in the effort to get appointments, one of your major considerations is your own travel time. Group your prospects on a geographic basis.

   Put the name, address and phone number of each prospect on a 3 x 5 card.

2. *Mail a letter.* The letter is not intended to sell a product or a service. The letter is not even intended to sell an appointment. The letter should serve four purposes exclusively:

   A. The letterhead identifies your firm and the nature of your business.
   B. The signature identifies you.
   C. The letter alerts the prospect to the fact that you will phone.
   D. The letter plants the feeling that you can offer the reader a benefit.

   The letter, in most cases, need be no longer than two sentences:

Dear Mr. Crimson,

Something that can be of great benefit to you has come to my attention. In the next day or two I will phone to see when we can meet.

Cordially,
Joe Seller

Each letter should be individually typed and hand signed. The 3 x 5 cards from which the addressing was done should carry a notation of the date of mailing.

3. *Telephone.* Exactly 48 hours after the letters are mailed the telephone call should be made. 24 hours may be too soon for there may be some delay in delivery. 72 hours may be too late for maximum effectiveness because the letter is so brief, and says so little, it may have been forgotten. *Do not depart from the 48 hour timing.*

This is the exact language you should use when you phone . . .

Mr. Crimson? (Wait for acknowledgment)

This is Joe Seller of the XYZ Company. You just had a letter from me.

Mr. Crimson, when would be the better time for us to meet . . . 10:20 a week from Thursday, or would 4:10 that Friday afternoon be better for you?

Analyze that brief message.

After establishing that fact that you had your prospect on the phone, the first thing you did was to identify yourself and your firm. Next you *told* him . . . *you did not ask* . . . that he just received a letter from you. Had you asked . . . in truth or as a stall . . . he might have told you that he had not received the letter and you would become involved in a fruitless and needless conversation.

Then you asked for a choice to two appointments.

The choices are out of the ordinary. One unusual aspect is that the suggested dates are nearly two weeks off. This has several advantages for you. While there is a natural reluctance for people to agree to making appointments with salesmen they don't know, it is immensely easier for them to agree to something that is off in the future than to something immediate. Secondly, the long-term suggestion implies that you must be busy and successful. People like to deal with successful men. Finally, most people cannot lie easily and quickly and it is difficult for them to pretend that they will be busy that far ahead.

The other unusual aspect of the choice you offered is that you mentioned 10:20 in the morning and 4:10 in the afternoon. Once again you appear to be unusually busy. The odd times also suggest that your visit will be brief. And if the person called truly is so busy that he has solid schedules that far ahead, he is given the feeling that these odd hour suggestions will enable him to sandwich you in between two others.

Frequently prospects will ask, "What is it about?"

If you could make sales on the phone, you wouldn't be asking for an appointment, *so don't be trapped into making the effort.* And don't make the mistake of telling just a few highlights for to do so is to invite the prospect to make a yes or no decision on the basis of insufficient knowledge, which isn't fair to him or to you.

Answer in this manner . . .

Mr. Crimson, I sincerely wish it were possible to save your time and mine by telling the story on the phone, but without keeping you on the phone for an inconsiderate length of time I couldn't do it justice. When we meet and I can show you and tell you what I have in mind, I can cover it in less than fifteen minutes. Would a week from Thursday be good for you, or do you prefer that Friday afternoon?

There will be other questions. *Always end your replies with the choice of dates.*

Do not insist. While it is instinctive and perfectly natural for cold prospects to hesitate and to toss out a few obstacles before agreeing to a firm date, some people you call will firmly refuse. You'll soon learn to recognize the hesitancy in the voices of the former and the rigidity in the voices of the latter. With those who are hesitant counter their stalls and questions and press for appointments. With those who are rigid, however, bow out gracefully and move along to your next prospect.

If, through persistence, you should manage to get agreement from some who are really opposed to a meeting, you will find that you have wasted your time when you keep the date. They will be resentful and antagonistic. Always remember that good prospecting consists of eliminating poor prospects and finding good ones.

While you are phoning, you will have your 3 x 5 cards in front of you. When you get an appointment, immediately note the day and time.

4. *Scheduling.* Plan to mail your letters every Monday and Tuesday. You will make your phone calls to the Monday group on Wednesdays ... to the Tuesday group on Thursdays. Following this schedule will avoid having your letters arrive on Mondays, the heaviest mail day of the week, and will make it unnecessary for you to do any phoning on Fridays, the day when many people are least receptive to interruptions.

How many letters you will mail each Monday and Tuesday will have to be determined by experimentation. Start by mailing 50 each on those two days.

In time you may find that you can mail fewer in order to get the number of appointments you can handle properly. Or you may learn that you should mail in greater quantity. You will find that the phone calls will go very quickly and that you will become more proficient with the phone with practice. If you are not accustomed to using the phone for prospecting, this phase of the program will be difficult at first. With time, however, you will learn to relax, to speak in an unhurried, pleasant manner. You will learn how to make friends over the phone. That is when this program will reach the height of its effectiveness.

5. *Reminders.* Since you are making appointments 19 days to weeks ahead, don't depend on the efficiency or the memory of your prospects. The day after you make your appointments mail this memo or postcard:

Dear Mr. Crimson,

I enjoyed meeting you on the phone yesterday and look forward to seeing you in person at 10:20 in the morning, Thursday, November 14th.

Cordially,
Joe Seller

You may wonder why the initial letter is part of this program if you are going to telephone to ask for an appointment. Testing has shown that the letter is vital. Three times as many people will accept appointments when the letter is used as opposed to making the phone calls without the use of the letter.

When a prospect gets a phone call from a total stranger, without forewarning, he is uneasy and suspicious. While the salesman is talking the prospect's mind is occupied with questions as to who the salesman is and why he is calling. The advance letter eliminates these hindrances. The call is expected. The prospect knows who you are, what firm you represent, what business you are in and he has been advised that you want to see him to offer something that may be beneficial to him.

PREVIOUS CONTACTS

When you write to people you know asking for an appointment, your approach must be different. The degree of intimacy you have with such people will, naturally, have a strong bearing on how you express yourself.

A letter to established customers or to prospects you have visited before can be written in this manner . . .

Dear Mr. Gold,

I'm looking forward to seeing you again soon for I have some things to tell you that can be of great value to you.

The most fascinating part of my work is meeting and talking with so many different people for I always learn something. Recently I have run into some novel ideas that you may be able to adopt quite profitably.

I will phone in the next day or two to ask when it will suit your convenience for me to drop in.

Cordially,

You would not send such a letter, of course, before you were prepared to present some practical new ideas to the people on your list.

But what the letter says is true. You are constantly exposed to the opportunity to see, hear and read about new concepts in the use of their
products or services. Each firm or individual you deal with has a slightly
different application for whatever you sell. Your company and your
company's resources, trade publications, industry meetings and conventions all bring forward ideas that make excellent sales tools. There is no
more certain way to win appointments than to merit them by offering
ideas.

If you have established a good relationship with a very busy person
who is difficult to see, this letter can be highly effective . . .

Dear Jack,

The first time you see fifteen minutes open on your calendar, please
call me.

I have some news for you that I think you'll relish.

My warmest regards.

Cordially,

Again, such a letter must be used only when you actually have some
real news to present . . . news that is calculated to be valued by the
prospect or customer.

How You Found the Prospect

Names of prospective customers come to you from a variety of sources.
If you simply have compiled a list of logical interest groups, the source
of the names will play no part in the letters you write. When names come
to you from customers or friends, however, you can use that added advantage.

Dear Mr. Green,

Frank Blue suggested that I get in touch with you.

I've had the pleasure of dealing with Frank for many years. A few days ago he mentioned your name to me and said that he thought you would be interested in learning about my firm, its products and the services that I offer.

From all Frank has said it will be a privilege for me to meet you.

I'll phone you in the next few days with the hope that you can find time for me to drop in.

Sincerely,

The first thing Mr. Green will see is the name of his friend, Frank Blue. You can be certain that he will read the letter with interest. The letter avoids any detail about what you sell. It makes no effort to sell anything but the meeting. The tone reduces any of the negative feelings a man might have when asked to meet a new salesman.

Some prospect names will be gathered from items in your daily paper. You might, for example, read that Mr. India has been promoted to the position of executive vice-president of a local firm that could do business with you.

Dear Mr. India,

My heartiest congratulations on being named executive vice-president of the Hearty Company. It is a great tribute to have your skills and your efforts recognized in such a manner.

Undoubtedly you will be unusually busy taking over your new responsibilities. In a few weeks, after you have had time to make the adjustment, I would welcome the opportunity to meet you. I have some ideas that you may find to be particularly valuable and I'd like to present them to you.

I will phone just after the first of the month. The best of good luck.

Sincerely,

Your letterhead tells Mr. India what business you are in. The appreciation of his qualities and the consideration displayed in your letter cannot fail to make him well disposed toward you. He is in a new role and, as is so often the case, may be looking for quick opportunities to make changes. Before you call him, he may call you.

The men in your community who are the leaders in their businesses or professions, in civic and charitable activities, may be the most attractive prospects of all. Merely because they are so well-known and so highly placed, many salesmen avoid approaching them. They assume that such men are besieged by the competition and that hard and fast alliances must exist. This may or may not be true, and it never hurts to try.

> Dear Mr. Jade,
>
> There is no doubt in my mind that one reason why you have such great achievements to your credit is that you are a man who is open to and welcomes ideas.
>
> I have an idea that could be of great interest to you.
>
> It would be a privilege to meet you, Mr. Jade, and I will be most grateful if I could have a fifteen minute appointment.
>
> > Sincerely,

The letter is flattering but it is not insincere. Important men relish ideas and have found their way to the top through ideas. This letter, you will notice, ends differently from some on earlier pages. Most of the others closed with the statement that you would phone for an appointment. In this case you are addressing yourself to a man who probably is difficult to reach by phone. If he is impressed by your letter and you did promise to phone, he will see no need to take action. The absence of any mention of further action on your part, therefore, can prompt him to tell his secretary to phone or write to you. If you have no response within a week, you still can try to reach him by phone.

In Summary . . . .

When using letters to win selling appointments, these are the key points to keep in mind:

1. When you offer a well-known tangible, capitalize on the reader's probable familiarity with the product.
2. If your product is little known, work hard to arouse curiosity and desire.

3. Excite the reader's imagination when offering an intangible.
4. In all appointment-seeking letters make the desired easy and, as often as possible, show that you will make the next move.
5. Plan a series of appointment-seeking letters . . . not just one.
6. The most successful appointment-winning technique is the combination of a letter and a phone call.
   A. Prepare a list.
   B. Mail a very brief letter.
   C. Phone.
   D. Offer a choice of dates.
   E. Don't be overly insistent.
   F. Mail reminders.
7. Be certain to refer to previous contacts when writing to people you know.
8. When writing to referred leads, capitalize on the referrer's name.
9. Use the news columns to find prospects.

7

Letters Seeking Referrals

As a salesman you constantly are looking for new prospects. The great majority of successful salesmen agree that the finest prospects are those that are introduced by satisfied customers. Once a customer has been motivated to provide some referrals that same customer can be cultivated to become a source of many leads . . . a center of influence. But the original motivation and the development of that customer as a center of influence demands thoughtful handling.

Beginning salesmen generally are surprised at the willingness of customers to be cooperative when asked for names of friends, family members and business associates. But people are willing . . . if approached with knowledge and understanding.

Most referral work is done while the salesman is with his customers, but letters can be used with great effectiveness.

SOMETHING GOOD HAS HAPPENED

An ideal time to ask a customer for help is when something you have done or something your company has done is particularly pleasing to the customer. He has reason to feel grateful and his enthusiasm for you is at a high level. He can recommend you without any mental reservations.

Dear Mr. Pace,

Your warm praise and enthusiasm for the recent booklet we printed for you delighted me. I made a point of telling everyone who worked on the job about your generous praise. You'd have enjoyed their reactions . . . the biggest smiles you ever saw.

Years ago I went to a young dentist. He had a favorite expression each time he was about to drill . . . "If this hurts, tell me—if it doesn't, tell others."

Since the work we do for you "doesn't hurt," I'd appreciate your help in telling others.

On Thursday morning I'll be in your office with the type proofs on your up-dated manual. If, while I'm there, you would do me the great favor of giving me the names of two or three people who might benefit by learning about our facilities and know-how, I will be extremely grateful.

See you Thursday.

Cordially,

————————

Dear Mr. Pence,

This afternoon I got the word that a check, in full settlement of your claim, was mailed to you. I'm certain that you are as pleased as I am that my company handled it so quickly and efficiently.

While it is unfortunate that you had occasion to make a claim, it did give you the opportunity to learn that you can have peace of mind about the type of protection you've wisely adopted.

There can be a lot of satisfaction in sharing good things with good friends. I've put three introduction cards and an addressed and stamped envelope in with this letter. If you will take a moment to write the names and addresses of three friends on those cards, and mail them back to me, I'll be deeply grateful. There's a good chance that your friends will be grateful too.

My warmest regards.

Cordially,

————————

Dear Mr. Adler,

Yesterday afternoon I was in your plant and spent a few hours checking over the installation and offering some ideas and help to the operators. They're good people and they know their jobs well.

I hope that you are as pleased with the new equipment as they are.

Mr. Alder, the chances are that installations of this type would also be ideal for some of your business friends. Most of my sales come from customers introducing me to potential users. If you know one or two people who might see the benefits you saw in our equipment, I'd be deeply grateful if you'd tell me who they are.

Next week I'll phone to see who has come to mind.

Cordially,

The three letters you just read contain some of the key elements in making successful requests for referrals:

1. They remind the reader why he should feel good about you and the firm you represent.
2. They stress the potential benefits to friends.
3. They make it physically easy to grant the request.
4. Either openly or subtly they play to the ego of the customer who will feel good about helping somebody.

The letter to Mr. Pence embodies the use of introduction cards and a business reply envelope. The introduction card is used with great success in many fields of selling. It can be quite simple ...

To: ....

(Address) ....

This will introduce John Jones of the ABC Company. I think you'll be interested in hearing his story.

....

Filling in and signing such a card creates a minimum of resistance. It doesn't make any claims or promises. It doesn't even recommend. The signer does no more than say that his friend may be interested in the presentation.

TRANSMITTING INFORMATION

Another opportunity to make your bid for some leads is when you have occasion to forward information to a customer.

Dear Mr. Laddenmill,

Yesterday or today you probably received the custodian bank's confirmation of the share purchase made for your company's profit-sharing plan. My copy arrived this morning.

Although I'll be in touch with you from time to time, I will miss the close contact we had while the details of the plan were being resolved. Thank you for making them so pleasant and so stimulating.

You can do me an important favor, Mr. Laddenmill. It could mean a great deal to me were you to pave the way for me to meet two or three of your friends who might welcome the chance to explore the creation of similar plans for their own companies. Just as you recognized and embraced the many benefits, they might also.

I'll check with Miss Dawson to learn when you will have a few free moments one day next week and I'll drop by.

Sincerely,

GIVE SOMETHING

Thoughtfulness leads to thoughtfulness. If you have something extra that you can give to a customer, you have created a perfect atmosphere for asking a favor.

Dear Mr. Marcey,

You'll be particularly interested in the enclosed Financial Planning Study. It is devoted to a subject you've talked about at some of our meetings. I hope you find it valuable.

Your mutual fund investment has been performing handsomely up to this time, and I'm sure that you and Mrs. Marcey are well pleased with the program you adopted.

It occurred to me, Mr. Marcey, that you must have some family members and friends who would welcome the opportunity to learn about this method of investing. They, like you, probably have long-term financial needs and might be interested in exploring steps they can take to prepare for those needs.

I'd enjoy meeting and working with them and would deeply appreciate your making such meetings possible. In the early part of next week I'll phone to see if you have two or three people in mind. There's a good possibility that you'll have the satisfaction of knowing that you helped them while helping me.

Cordially,

————————

Dear Mrs. Glade,

Your living room must glow with the beautiful furniture you chose. Because I know you'll want to keep it glowing, I'm going to drop by on my way home in the next day or two with a gift.

We use a furniture polish that keeps our display furniture at its peak of beauty, and I'd like you to have a bottle of it.

Will you do me one great favor?

Between now and the time I bring the polish, please jot down the names and addresses of a few friends who may be thinking of refurnishing or moving into a new home or apartment. I'd love to meet them and to offer my help.

Sincerely,

In both cases the items given were logical . . . tied to the product or service involved . . . and, of course, to the customers' interests.

The two letters point up another important factor in seeking referrals. The letter to Mr. Marcey speaks of two or three names. The letter to Mrs. Glade refers to "a few friends." Without these modest limitations the request can bring to the customer's mind the idea that he is being asked to go to a great deal of trouble. When you are explicit, however, as to your desire for a minimum number of names, the negative reaction is eliminated.

Help Customers to Think of Names

Your customers lack your experience in determining who are and who are not good prospects. Their desire to help you may be genuine; but if they have to indulge in some heavy concentration in the effort to comply, their good intentions may evaporate. It is good practice, when possible, to pinpoint the people or the types of people you would like to meet.

Dear Mr. Cauley,

One of the most satisfying aspects of my activities is the chance they give me to meet fine people. Thanks for adding to the pleasure I find in my work.

During some of our conversations you mentioned two of your associates, Mr. Collings and Mr. Mowbry. Had these gentlemen walked into your office while we were together I'm sure you, unhesitatingly, would have introduced us. Will you do that now?

I look forward to meeting them and, as in your case, I may be able to offer them some ideas that they'll be glad to have.

I'll be in touch with you one day next week.

Cordially,

———————

Dear Mr. Holden,

You and that new car of yours know each other by now, and I'm confident that you are enjoying it thoroughly.

I also suspect that you've heard some envious admiration from a number of your friends. If I could learn who some of those envying admirers are, I would be most grateful.

I'll phone you one evening this week to see if you have a few names for me.

Gratefully,

Your ability to name names has clear advantages. With this in mind look for and encourage the opportunities to pick up names when you are with your customers. Write them down as soon as you have left a customer's office or home. They are valuable assets.

SINCERE COMPLIMENTS ARE POWERFUL LEVERS

If you truly like a customer and enjoy being with him, the message comes through. We usually can sense the honest feelings of those we meet. Nothing pleases us more than to be liked and appreciated. If you have developed a customer you really like, don't hesitate to say so. You will not be regarded as a hypocritical flatterer saying nice things solely for your own advantage.

Dear Mr. and Mrs. Keeter,

Do all of your friends love your new home as much as you do? I'll bet they do.

Joining the two of you in the search for just the right home was fun.

Do you know anyone who is interested in buying or selling a home now? If you do, I'd appreciate learning who they are. Invariably I work harder and succeed more often when representing nice people and I'm sure that any friends of yours are nice people.

I'll drop by one day soon to see if you have any tips for me.

Cordially,

WHEN CUSTOMERS HAVE BECOME GOOD FRIENDS

Regardless of the subject, when you write to a customer who has become a good friend, the letter should reflect the relationship. Friends are glad to grant favors if you tell them what and tell them how.

Dear Marty,

You could do something great for me.

Next week, when you are at the convention, you'll be seeing a lot of old friends and making some new ones. A number of the men you'll see operate stores like yours in other cities and within my territory.

It could mean a lot to me if you'd tell some of these folks about what you've been able to do with my line . . . about the kind of help and cooperation you get.

Next time I'm in I'll pick up the names of those you think are interested and I'll go to work.

Hope you enjoy the convention and come back loaded with new ideas that will make your great store even greater.

My best, Marty . . .

Referrals from Non-Customers

You are a businessman and every time you make a presentation you have made an investment. You have invested your precious time, your energy and, in many cases, some expense. As a businessman you should try to get a return from any investment you make. All salesmen will encounter some situations where they do not make a sale but come away with the knowledge that they made a favorable impression.

Dear Mr. Ortend,

My sincerest thanks for seeing me yesterday. Even though no business resulted I hope that some of the ideas we discussed will, in one way or another, prove to be of value to you.

You told me that you could see the broad benefits in the program and wished you had known about it before you had committed yourself to your present course.

After leaving you it occurred to me that you probably have some friends or associates who are in position to take advantage of the program. I'd appreciate being able to meet and present the idea to them.

Please use the other side of this letter to jot down the names and addresses of any people you know who might be interested in having the information. I'll be most grateful. The enclosed stamped and addressed envelope will bring the names back to me.

Many thanks.

Sincerely,

MAKING CUSTOMERS CENTERS OF INFLUENCE

At the start of this chapter, the development of centers of influence was mentioned. A center of influence is a person who proves to be a continuing source of good referrals. Any center of influence a salesman develops is like a gold mine. Each time he goes to the mine he can carry away wealth.

A center of influence seldom springs up spontaneously. It must be found and carefully cultivated. It starts with the first referral.

When somebody gives you a few names of people you can call on, with his blessings, he was moved to do so because he has become interested in you and because he is interested in the people whose names he provided. He is human and, as such, has curiosity. Your successful appeal to him for names and his decision to grant your request form two parts of a three-part story. He wants to know how the story ended. If you fail to end the suspense, you probably have closed the door to any further help from that source. Make a mission of keeping your customers advised as to the outcome of any referrals they give you.

Dear Mr. Jappa,

Last Tuesday I had lunch with Frank Paul. Many thanks for introducing us. He's a fine, intelligent man and I'm delighted that I know him.

As you anticipated, Mr. Paul was quite interested in our services and immediately saw how they might solve a problem for him. He has arranged a meeting of his department heads so that I can describe our offer to the full group and answer their questions. It is an exciting opportunity and I'm full of confidence as to the outcome.

I'm sure I don't have to tell you how grateful I am. As soon as I know what the decision is, I'll let you know.

Cordially,

––––––––––

Dear Mr. Sullivan,

John James and I had a long and interesting session at his home last night.

We talked about his insurance needs for nearly three hours. At this time it doesn't look as though he and I will be doing any business, but he's a fine man and I'm glad that I met him. He had some things to say about you that you would have been proud to hear.

My sincerest thanks for bringing us together.

My warm regards.

Cordially,

––––––––––

Dear Mr. DuForret,

Saturday morning I picked up Mrs. Leans and took her for a demonstration ride in one of our convertibles.

Now she owns it.

A million thanks to you.

Cordially,

In Summary . . . .

Referrals and the development of centers of influence can be your most important means of building sales. Letters can be of major assistance if they are based on . . .

1. Reminders of why they should like you and your company.
2. The potential benefit to the customer's friends.

3. The ease of granting your request.
4. An appeal to the reader's ego.
5. Something good that has happened.
6. The transmittal of information.
7. Giving something extra.
8. Help in thinking of appropriate names.
9. Sincere compliments.
10. Keeping customers advised as to the outcome of their introductions.

8

Letters Offering Extra Services to Customers

The comment has been made that once you convert a prospect to a customer, he becomes everybody else's prospect. Having an established customer is like owning a gold mine. The discovery and bringing some gold to market is just a beginning. Handled properly, you have a source of continuing riches.

It is dangerously easy to take a well-established, seemingly satisfied customer for granted, no matter how strong the relationship may be. You do have competitors and some of them may be eager to go to great extremes to lure a good customer away from you. The surest way to safeguard against such losses is to be continuously alert for opportunities to offer each customer extra services that will demonstrate your dedication to him and his best interests.

Many of the extra services you can offer may be explained through letters. Here, as in many other cases, a letter can be superior to word of mouth. The very fact that you took the time and trouble to write a letter . . . as opposed to conversation . . . gives the offer an added measure of importance. A letter is a matter of record, evidencing your absolute intention of rendering the service in question. A letter can be studied and restudied and can be shown to others in your customer's organization.

PERSONAL SERVICES

The most impressive extra services you can offer are those that involve your personal time and effort. You are telling your customer of your readiness to roll up your sleeves to go to work for him.

Your offer to conduct sales training sessions for a customer's sales force usually will win grateful acceptance. Before making such an offer you will, of course, be fully prepared to handle the task in an impressive, practical manner. It may be your decision to devote the session to pure sales training, avoiding any commercialism. If, however, you want and need some emphasis on the products or services your company offers, make it clear that this is your intention, thus avoiding any later resentment.

Dear Mr. Coftus,

Here's an idea you'll probably welcome.

You'll probably agree that the greater the knowledge of your salesmen the more productive they can be.

I have developed a 90 minute training program. It is based on the great variety of sales approaches, demonstration techniques and closing methods I've had the unique opportunity to observe while working with many dealers and salesmen in the electrical appliance field.

Sales methods have always held particular interest for me. When I see an outstanding salesman, I make a point of getting to know him well, observing him and analyzing his work.

One of the objectives of the meeting will be to motivate your people to want to become more professional in their sales efforts.

While our line will be mentioned, I can assure you that the session will be dedicated to improving their selling skills no matter what products or what lines they choose to sell.

Tell me when and where and I'll be delighted to conduct the meeting for your sales force.

Cordially,

If what you sell through distributors is a subject that lends itself to group selling and group education, the offer to conduct public seminars on behalf of your customer can be unusually profitable to him, to you and to your company. Don't make the offer until you have developed a highly polished presentation and have tested it. No matter how much cooperation you provide, the customer will be required to expend a good deal of effort and money to attract the audience and to hold the meeting. If your presentation to the audience fails to produce results and to build up your customer's prestige, you may do more harm than good.

Dear Pete,

Here's a way to handle 128 hours of face-to-face presentation time in 2 hours.

It's simple arithmetic.

On average, it takes one of your salesmen an hour and a half to make a full, effective presentation to a prospect. You have 12 salesmen. If each of them makes presentations to 6 prospects, that adds up to 128 hours.

My suggestion is that you get each of your salesmen to invite 6 prospects to a 2 hour meeting. I'll handle the meeting, conducting a seminar that has proven to be immensely effective. The seminar, in actuality, is a carefully planned presentation. A lot of thought and investment have gone into its organization. I use a variety of visual aids to help people to understand better and to be motivated more fully.

This has been done for other dealers in other cities, and the sales that follow have been substantial.

Before the seminar I'll conduct a meeting with your salesmen to train them on the most resultful follow-through methods, and I'll stay in town for three days after the seminar to be available to work with both salesmen and clients.

I'll phone you next week to discuss the details . . . to tell you how I'll cooperate in the handling of invitations to the meeting . . . the choice of the best time, place, and to decide when it should be scheduled.

It is an exciting opportunity for you and for your salesmen. And if the first seminar I conduct for you is as productive as I believe it will be, others can follow.

My best, Pete . . .

Offering your personal efforts to create well qualified leads for a customer can't fail to entice him and win his genuine appreciation. You are putting money in his pockets.

Dear Mr. Fanks,

You've got a thousand and one problems and I've got an idea that will reduce them to an even thousand.

As an important jobber, your men represent so many lines you can't hope to have any of them concentrate on one, such as mine, even though it represents unusually high profit margins for you.

Give me your okay and I'll take time out to conduct a city-wide survey to uncover genuinely interested prospects. The manner in which I'll work will embrace some effective pre-selling. The leads I'll turn over to you will be confined to people who have said that they are sincerely interested and want a demonstration.

All I want from you is the assurance that your people will know what I'm doing . . . will recognize the value of the leads . . . will make the most of them by going to see those people fast.

You tell me the maximum number of leads your men can cover each week and I'll work accordingly.

After you've had time to give this idea some thought, and to do some checking with your people, I'll call on you and we can start rolling.

Cordially,

There are some extra service offers that will occur to you that may or may not prove acceptable. In the letter that follows, the salesman offers to make weekly inventory checks of his own products in the customer's stockrooms or warehouse. He may learn that this is contrary to the customer's policy. Unless you have knowledge of such a policy . . . and you sincerely believe it will be beneficial to the customer . . . don't hesitate to make the offer. Even if it is refused, you have put yourself on record as a man who is willing to exert himself to be helpful.

Dear Henry,

I've decided to take a new job.

From now on I'll be working for you . . . one day each week.

Yesterday you suddenly found that you were out of our family-size pack in your warehouse and in two of your stores. Even though we were able to rush replacements out in a hurry some sales were lost and some of your customers were disappointed.

With all the items you have in your warehouse, that sort of emergency is bound to come up from time to time.

With your permission, therefore, I'm more than willing to take the responsibility of taking inventory of our products in your warehouse every Monday afternoon.

It will take some reshuffling of my own schedules but that's a small price for me to pay for the opportunity to spare you the problem of either over-supply or under-supply.

I'll phone you Monday morning to see if you'd like to have me take the job.

Cordially,

You and Your Company

Some of the extra services you may propose reflect your own willingness to do something for the customer, combined with your company's full cooperation. It is an impressive combination that is calculated to win excellent good will.

Dear Bert,

How would you like to make next month the biggest sales month you've ever had?

I think I can help you to make that possible.

Over the years I've seen a good many sales contests conducted in our field, I've learned what works and what doesn't work. On the basis of that experience and observation I have developed one that is handsomely suited to your organization.

The boss and I had a long discussion about my plans and I've sold him on the idea of having our company contribute prizes that will make your boys roll up their sleeves and sell as they never have before.

Interested?

You're a hard man to reach on the phone, so call me collect and I'll give you the whole story.

My best . . .

Ideas Can Be Invaluable

Your desire to give customers ideas that can help them will always get a warm reception. The offer demonstrates your devotion to their interests and this is particularly true if the idea is one that has no relationship to your selling him anything additional.

Dear Lou,

Congratulations on that new series of ads you're running. They're imaginative and strikingly executed.

As is true of all effective advertising, the real power behind the series is your merchandising idea. Completely coordinated ensembles of clothing for men is a concept that has been publicized before, but you have taken a giant step forward in terms of completeness and variety.

Perhaps you'll welcome a thought I've had to carry the idea a bit further.

Your display windows have tied in with your newspaper ads, by showing various ensembles and they are well done. But men passing by expect to see men's clothing in the windows of a men's clothing store . . . and that's what they still see. Unless they are bent on window shopping, they may not get the picture.

My thought is to have your window dresser use your windows to catch "the man who runs" by featuring other things that go together . . . ham and eggs . . . bread and butter . . . Adam and Eve (mannikins appropriately garbed) . . . hearts and flowers, etc. In the center you'd exhibit a typical ensemble with a card devoted to your theme.

If the thought is helpful . . . great. If not, I repeat my congratulations on your imaginative approach and hope it sells a lot of merchandise and wins many new customers for you.

My best . . .

Dear Larry,

Now that all the grief and frenzy are over, I hope things have settled back to normal for you.

Your problem led me to some serious thinking. As you know far too well, the finest of press equipment and the best of printers still can't rule out freak accidents and breakdowns such as you just experienced. Having your big press out of action for almost a week is tragically costly in terms of productive time lost and holding customer good will.

I have a thought.

There are seven plants within a seventy-five mile radius with that same press. Each is subject to the unexpected and the tolls such incidents exact. Starting with you, I'm contacting each owner to suggest an "emergency take-over agreement."

It is simple. If any one of you ever is forced to shut down on that press, the others agree to take-over any jobs scheduled to be run at that time.

If the idea makes sense to you, and to some of the others, let's have a meeting and work out the details.

Cordially,

_____

Dear George,

Yesterday I stole something for you.

The constant traveling my job demands gets tough at times but it also offers some resounding rewards. The greatest of the rewards is the opportunity it gives me to see how different merchants handle selling and merchandising problems in different ways. It is a great education that never quits.

And yesterday I saw a merchandising idea that is terriffic . . . terriffic because it works like magic. Seeing it, I thought immediately of you. It fits you, your store, your community.

So I stole the idea for you.

My friend who originated it couldn't care less and said so. He's four hundred miles away, so you are hardly a competitor. He even gave me a full set of the literature and internal forms involved.

While you and I seldom have more than a half hour together when I call, this time I suggest you set aside a good two hours because I have a lot to tell you. I'll be in your town a week from Tuesday. Suppose I come to your place at eleven. We can work in your office for an hour and finish up the planning on the tablecloth at lunch.

I'll phone ahead to be sure you were able to block out the time.

Cordially,

COMPANY SERVICES

From time to time your company will make extra services available to your customers. Your use of a personal letter to dramatize such opportunities has two worthy advantages. First, it highlights the offer and, second, it ties you to the offer to a greater degree than if you simply tell people about it.

Dear Jack,

You and Paul have been great producers for us. But I'm a hard man to satisfy and I'd like to see you do much more.

Therefore . . .

"You are cordially invited."

The thought is this . . . each Wednesday our investment advisory committee meets to make decisions about the fund's investments. I've had the privilege of attending some of those meetings and they are completely fascinating. When you see men of the stature we have on that committee probing the reports made by the heads of our research organization . . . when you listen to their observations and keenly analytical conclusions . . . when you become aware of their closeness to leading financial and industrial figures across the Nation . . . you come away feeling that you've really had an insider's view of what makes our whole economy tick.

You also come away with immense pride and satisfaction in the thoughtful, prudent, knowledgeable way our shareholders' interests are being represented.

That's why I want you and Paul to come to one of those meetings.

I've already been told that you'll be more than welcome. So if you'll just tell me when you can make the trip, I'll complete the arrangements for your stay here.

Make it soon, Jack.

My warmest regards . . .

———————

Dear Marty,

Take a good look at the material I'm enclosing with this letter. Look at it hard enough and you'll see the color of money.

The firm recently created a new direct mail campaign that our dealer friends can put to work. It's been tested in four cities and does a great job.

Ordinarily, when something like this comes along, I send samples to my customers and ask how many they want . . . and that's that. But this campaign deserves more than that, and so do you.

I'm going to be certain that you get all the benefits this campaign can bring you. You're busy with a thousand details a day, so I plan to take on my shoulders the detail of getting this mailing out for you in the ideal manner.

Marty, just send me a copy of your mailing list and I'll take care of everything. The addressing, inserting, sealing and metering will be done for you. The only cost to you will be the postage. But, even more important, the real power in this mailing lies in the follow-through of your salesmen. So . . . before the pieces are mailed, I'll be in your shop to have a real session with your men so that each will see the potential and will know exactly how to capitalize on the campaign.

I'm tickled to have this chance to do something for you, Marty, that can mean so much to your sales and profits.

Send me the list and let's go.

Cordially,

———————

Dear Art,

Unless you are opposed to pretty girls, I'd like to bring one to you.

Don't burn this letter until you read further.

The girl I'm talking about is a professional demonstrator of our products, and I simply want to bring her to your store for a full week to help you to win new customers.

I've been given the opportunity to make this offer to a few customers and, naturally, I hurried to make this special opportunity available to you.

Mrs. Swanson, the demonstrator, is unusually capable and has a wonderful sales personality. And she *is* pretty. She'll be a real asset to you and you'll be delighted with the way sales of our products will zoom for you . . . not only while she's there, but many of the new users she'll develop will be consistent repeaters.

When would you like Mrs. Swanson to come?

Cordially,

In Summary . . . .

It pays to cement your relationships with existing customers by constantly seeking ways to offer them extra services. One of the most effective ways of bringing your offers to peoples' attention is by using thoughtfully composed letters. You can use letters to announce extra services based on . . .

1. Things you will do.
2. Things you and your company will do.
3. Ideas that customers can use.
4. Company services.

9

Letters of Appreciation to Established Customers

The unexpected will pay dividends. A new customer takes a letter of thanks for granted. It is customary. An old customer who has given you an unusually big order will be pleased by a thank you letter, but it won't surprise him. But a letter of thanks . . . just out of the blue . . . not inspired by any current activity . . . will make a deep and lasting impression.

Stop to think about it for a moment and you'll readily see that your long-term, loyal customers are the people most deserving of your gratitude. They are the bed-rock sources of your income. They are the easiest people to serve, for they know you, your firm, your goods and services and you know a great deal about them. You know, too, that they are constantly subjected to competitive lures . . . but they continue to buy from you.

But it can be dangerous to take loyalty for granted and to assume that nothing can destroy it. Strong ties can be made even stronger. A buyer's defenses against the urgings of your competitors can be reinforced. The feeling of friendship and good will that you enjoy from your long-term customers can be enhanced. And one of the easiest ways to accomplish these desirable enrichments is to write letters.

Everyone wants to be appreciated. You may thoroughly appreciate your best customers, but they won't know the extent of your appreciation if you keep it to yourself. A totally unnecessary letter, written from the heart, will say more and will be better received than a costly good will gift.

PURE GRATITUDE

Many "I think you're great" letters can and should be confined to pure thanks for continuing patronage.

Dear Mark,

Last night I came home from a three week trip and felt very triumphant because of the number of new accounts I had opened. This morning I was writing my report for the boss and suddenly I realized something.

Here I was reveling in finding some new customers when the greatest thing I have is loyal, long-term customers like you.

It didn't take much thought for me to recognize the fact that having one great, consistent customer such as you, Mark, is better than opening dozens of new accounts.

I just wanted to tell you how much I do appreciate our long and happy relationship. Thank you.

My best . . .

———————

Dear Mrs. Grace,

As you know, we have a valuable inventory of furs, but we have something I consider to be of far greater value. We have your continuing patronage.

You've been an appreciated customer of mine for a long time, Mrs. Grace, and I just had the irresistible desire to write this brief note to tell you how warmly and deeply I appreciate the privilege of serving you.

Sincerely,

———————

Dear Harry,

I wonder if you realize how long ago you opened your account with me?

During the past weekend I was doing some wool gathering, thinking about people I've met and worked with over the years . . . the people who have made it possible for me to have a pleasant home where I can sit back and enjoy my relaxation.

I've had the pleasure of dealing with you for nearly twenty years. Thank you, Harry, for your continuing loyalty. I am more grateful than I can say.

My best . . .

———————

Dear Mr. Marrin,

My heartfelt thanks.

While driving to work this morning, I was thinking about the thank you letters I should send to two new customers. Then it suddenly occurred to me that while saying thanks to folks who just bought from me may be good business, I never have taken the time to express my deeply sincere appreciation to you for your loyalty over the years.

I suppose I'm no more guilty than most people. We are so concerned with day-to-day business needs we seldom take time out to show the great gratitude we feel for our most important business friends . . . those who keep coming back and who thoughtfully send others to us.

I am grateful.

Cordially,

———————

Dear Mr. Champer,

This is not to tell you about a sale . . . some new merchandise . . . or new fashion notes.

As a matter of fact it is about something we've had for a long time . . . your good will and greatly appreciated loyalty.

That is the only reason for this letter. You've been a regular customer of mine for a long time and I simply wanted to say that I am very grateful.

Cordially,

Gratitude Plus Praise

If there is something a customer can be praised for beyond sheer loyalty, by all means include your sincere praise in your thank you letter. Let him know that you recognize and admire his good qualities.

Dear Mr. Harmon,

My admiration is the reason for this letter.

For seventeen years you have faithfully maintained your family protection policy in a businesslike manner. On three occasions over that period of time, you have reviewed your program and have made realistic additions.

Part of my work is to contact policyholders who have forgotten the importance of sound insurance protection and have become careless about this vital foundation for the future welfare of themselves and their families.

To keep myself aware of those who need help and counsel, I constantly review the records of all my clients. While doing that today, I read your record and just couldn't resist the impulse to tell you how much I admire your precise and intelligent approach to your financial well-being.

Cordially,

Gratitude Plus Sell

Handled carefully, your letters of appreciation can encompass more than your thanks. Subtly, you can strengthen a customer's reasons for continuing business. You can remind him of the things you do that probably have inspired long years of dealing. There may be occasions when such a letter can do a most effective job if you have reason to believe that a long-term relationship may be threatened by some outside influence.

Dear Charles,

There's an article in the current issue of one of the trade magazines about clients who are afflicted with "agency hop-itis." They change ad agencies as often as they change their shirts.

Some do it because they enjoy the bowing, scraping and entertaining that goes with solicitations from new agencies. Some do it wistfully hoping for fresh approaches and new ideas.

I've met a few of the people suffering with the disease. They've called me in to invite proposals, but I've shied away.

It is my conviction that the most rewarding relationship between an agency and a client is an enduring one . . . one that gives each the opportunity to better understand the other's viewpoint, objectives and methods of operation.

Reading the article led to an even greater appreciation of you and your understanding of the real values of agency—client relationships.

It's a joy to work for you.

Cordially,

Dear Mr. Gerald,

It has been a good many years, but I clearly remember the first time I called on you. You told me at that time that you wanted a single source for all of your office supplies if you could find someone who would take a genuine interest in your needs and would give you good service.

Undoubtedly you have been approached by many other office supply firms. I'm sure some of them have made tempting price offers in their efforts to win your business. But the continuity of your dealings with me has never been disrupted.

It has been a source of great pleasure to me to see your business prosper and grow, and I've thoroughly enjoyed our fine relationship. Most of all, I want you to know how deeply I appreciate your loyalty.

Cordially,

———————

Dear Mrs. Benner,

I used your name this morning and I'm obeying the impulse to quote myself.

Our advertising agency people were in my office discussing our program for the next few months. I was asked if I could describe the type of customer I would like to attract. My answer was along these lines, "Mrs. John Benner has been a customer of ours for a long time. Whenever she needs any type of electrical appliance, she asks for our advice and help. Her loyalty over the years demonstrates her appreciation of the fact that genuine interest in a customer's needs, combined with good service, are more important than the possibility of saving a few dollars by price shopping."

Thank you, Mrs. Benner, for being that kind of customer.

Cordially,

———————

Dear Paul,

Yesterday a prospect refused to do business with me, and I want to thank you.

Don't think I have gone over the brink.

The prospect in question was very friendly and pleasant. He simply said that he had been dealing with one printer for many years . . . had always enjoyed fine service and good cooperation. He agreed that we might, on occasion, be able to underbid his regular printer, but he just wasn't interested in changing.

I left there a bit disappointed and thinking, "What a lucky guy that printer is to have such a loyal customer," when suddenly I realized how lucky I was to have a customer like you. I've handled all of your printing needs for a long time and I have a hunch that some of my competitors have heard a similar story from you.

Many thanks, Paul.

Gratefully,

In Summary . . . .

Letters of appreciation for continuing patronage can bolster customer loyalty substantially and can help to short-circuit competitive inducements. Your letters can . . .

1. Express simple gratitude.
2. Demonstrate respect in addition to gratitude.
3. Subtly resell yourself and your firm, while featuring your appreciation.

10

Letters to Be Mailed While You Are Away

In the relationship between a salesman and his customer, absence does not make the heart grow fonder. On the contrary, absence, which can be interpreted as a sign of indifference, can make the heart grow harder.

There are times and circumstances that make it impossible to see regular customers when you should . . . vacations, business trips and illnesses are the principal reasons. But letters from you can make a substantial difference. Your letters can explain why you haven't or won't show up and letters can serve to hold the loyalty of your customers.

When you write letters under such circumstances, you usually can find ways to do more than inform your customers about where you are. You can use those letters to reveal your interest in them and their needs. You can, in many cases, build anticipation for your next visit with them. Your letters, therefore, should be underscored by three factors . . . an explanation of your absence . . . a showing of your continuing interest . . . pre-selling in preparation for your next visit.

Vacation Letters

Since you are on vacation, give your letters a social tone. To a great extent they should be similar to letters you send to friends and members of the family.

Dear Rick,

The unwinding process is a week old now and I've reached the conclusion that vacations are here to stay. We're having a glorious, relaxed time.

I'm sure that Jerry is taking good care of you, for I briefed him well on the services you want and need. Be sure to stay on top of that Contoil merger possibility. It's due to firm up or be dropped any day now.

I'll call you when I get back on Monday, the 18th. Hope you're feeling as healthy as I do.

My best . . .

––––––––

Dear Mr. Richey,

If you've never been in this part of the country, I urge you to consider it for your next vacation. The climate is marvelous, the scenery is beautiful and there's plenty to do to fill the days with fun and interest.

Before I left, I filed that claim for you and I asked our Mr. Richardson to follow it through. If he hasn't already contacted you, he will just as quickly as he gets a reply from the home office. Rich is a top-notch man and you can rely on his attention to detail and his counsel completely.

Please be ready to work me hard when I get back. I'll need that to counteract the extra calories I've been absorbing. On July 12th I'll be back at the desk and raring to go.

Cordially,

––––––––

Dear Al,

Just came off the golf course and I refuse to tell you my score. But I sure enjoyed it. A great course with beautiful surroundings. I wish I could lure you up here for a few rounds. You'd love it.

If you run short of anything or any problems come up before I get back on the 25th, don't hesitate to call Mike collect. I asked him to keep an eye on your account while I was away and he'll do anything he can to help.

Hope business and your health are good, Al. I'll see you soon.

My best . . .

If you found it necessary to delay the start of your vacation in the interests of one of your clients, let him know that you did so without putting too much emphasis on your sacrifice.

Dear Mr. Patter,

One of the things that has made this vacation pure joy was that I saw your catalog come off the press the night before we left. I hope you're as delighted with it as I was. It should do an outstanding job for you.

Just after I get back on the 23rd, I'll come by to discuss that new mail order campaign with you. While driving out here, I had a few ideas that may add to the impact of the follow-up series.

Keep well and please give my best to Bud Eacher and Miss Low.

Cordially,

Postcards can serve to add interest to your correspondence with customers. This is particularly true when, before you leave on your vacation, you decide on a message you'd like to send to most, if not all, of your customers. It is a relatively easy matter to send away for postcards, write them, address and stamp them before you leave and then drop them in the mail after you've reached your destination. This has the added advantage of freeing you from business duties when you are trying to relax.

Dear Mr. Poulder,

I'm writing this card in one of the most charming hotel rooms I've ever enjoyed. This motor trip through southern France has been a tremendous experience. It's been a trip of discovery.

After I return, I must tell you about it in detail for I think you and Mrs. Poulder would love to visit some of the cities, inns and restaurants in this gorgeous area.

Cordially,

———————

Dear Mrs. Frank,

The picture on this postcard will show why my wife and I are so delighted with this place. I won the trip. My firm had a sales contest and I was one of the lucky ones.

Many thanks to you for the business you gave me. You helped make the trip possible. I hope that you and Mr. Frank will have the opportunity to enjoy this beautiful resort one day. It's great.

Gratefully,

CONVENTION AND TRADE SHOW LETTERS

Going away to attend a convention, trade show or seminar has potential advantages for the people you serve. You have taken the trip to broaden your knowledge . . . to fortify yourself with the most current information that might prove useful to your customers.

Even if these are short trips that don't seriously disrupt your schedules, it is a sound idea to let people know where you are, what you are doing and to show them what they may gain by your trip.

Dear Mr. Stummer,

I arrived in Chicago yesterday to attend the annual office equipment convention. The firm sent three of us here and I'm delighted that I was included.

The exhibits alone have made the trip worthwhile. Many great new products have been introduced at this show. Some of them will be particularly interesting to you and I'm anxious to get back to tell you about them.

Early next week I'll phone to see when you'll be free to see and hear about some of the items that can add to the economy and efficiency of your office operations.

Cordially,

────────

Dear Mr. Coldner,

Over the years I've attended a number of financial planning seminars and I've never failed to learn of some new approaches and new techniques.

I'm in my hotel room now with a stack of notes and published reports, getting them organized so that the mental decks will be clear for the sessions to follow.

When I return next week, I'd like to spend a little time with you to review some of the fresh ideas that may be particularly interesting to you.

Sincerely,

When You Are Ill

If you are out of circulation because of illness or an accident, your customers may or may not know why they haven't seen you. If you are strong enough to write letters, be equally strong in avoiding any bids for sympathy. Use letters simply to let your customers know why you haven't been around . . . that you have them in mind . . . that you are happy to do what you can for them while laid up . . . that you expect to be back soon.

Dear Miss Geniver,

You haven't seen me in the last two weeks for I've been on the sick list. Happily, the worst is over and I'm well on the road to recovery.

If you run short of any office supplies or need help in selecting or designing any new forms, please call George Hammer at my office. He's pinch hitting for me and will be more than glad to help you.

I'll be back on the job soon and will be by to see you.

Cordially,

Dear Mr. Groverton,

Normally, I would have been in to see you at this time of the year to review your mutual fund program with you and to offer any help you might need with your tax reporting. Unfortunately, I've been ill and I'm still confined to a box spring and mattress.

The phone is right at my bedside, so please don't hesitate to call me if I can do anything for you. The phone number is 641-2866. It would be a genuine pleasure to hear from you and to give you any counsel I can. The body's still weak, but the brain is crying for exercise.

Cordially,

In Summary . . . .

Whether your letters that explain your absence are from vacation spots, conventions or sickbeds there are certain key points to bear in mind . . .

1. Explain your absence with friendly warmth.
2. Show that you are thinking of their interests and needs.
3. Build anticipation for your next visit.
4. Tell them how they easily can get help while you are away.

11

Letters to Write Between Calls

Because of the size of his territory and the number of accounts he serves, a salesman often has to operate on a schedule that limits the number of times he can visit his active accounts. He has good reason to be concerned about what may be happening between calls. His customers may run out of his merchandise, have problems with service or merchandising and are constantly subjected to competitive offers.

Letters can play a potent role in the effort to circumvent problems created by the gap between calls.

The most important task your between-call letters can perform is to to keep you, your merchandise, your services and your dedication to each customer foremost in their minds. The solidifying of customer loyalty is a never ending job and if you aren't there, in person, to work on that invaluable but highly tentative element your letters are vital.

I'M DOING SOMETHING FOR YOU

When you face the problem of composing letters to customers that are calculated to build a sense of friendly obligation, you may find that your concentration on what can be said will lead you to doing things that otherwise may have been overlooked. There are countless things that can be done for good customers that do not require your being on the scene.

Dear Bud,

My regular visit to you is two weeks off but I just was given samples of our spring line of neckwear and I wanted you to have first crack at some of the most promising numbers.

I am putting some swatches of the new patterns in with this letter. These are exceptionally smart and right on top of the latest vogue. You can picture for yourself how handsomely they'll make up.

It's my hunch that these are going to be the most demanded items and I didn't want you, of all people, to be delayed in getting whatever supplies you may want. If you feel that these are for you, call the plant collect to place your order. I'll pick up your needs on the staples when we are together.

My best to the boys. See you soon.

Cordially,

———————

Dear Frank,

You asked me to keep my eyes open for an assistant buyer who has had a good, strong background with a store of your type.

Last night I head that Charrester's is going to have to close up. They've had a young fellow with them for about five years who always impressed me. He's smart, hard working and knows the business. His name is John Kling, and I think he's the man you want.

I didn't want to delay giving you this news until I see you again because there may be others who'll be interested in John. You can reach him direct by phoning or writing to him at Charrester's or, if you prefer, I'll be glad to speak to him for you.

My best . . .

———————

Dear Mr. Gluck,

As you know, I always make a check of your inventory when I call but my next scheduled trip is two weeks off. Since business has been particularly brisk this season, I'm a little concerned that you might run into some problems if that inventory check waits for me to get there.

Please have one of your people make a spot check. I'll phone you before noon on Friday to see if you need some replacements now. I suspect you will.

My warmest good wishes.

Cordially,

—————

Dear Jerry,

Last time we were together you asked me to give you a hand with your newspaper ads. It wasn't much of a hand for I'm a far cry from being an ad man.

Yesterday we had a meeting with our ad agency. When it ended, I buttonholed the agency representative and gave him a few of the ads you've been running. He's promised to have his people study them and come up with ideas, layouts and copy suggestions for you. And it won't cost you a dime.

I'll have them with me on my next trip. These folks are good and I'm sure you'll get some valuable help.

My best . . .

You'll observe that each of those four letters embraced the rendering of thoughtful, helpful services on your part. Some of those services may never have been performed had you not recognized the importance of letting your customers know that you have their interests at heart at all times.

OFFERING ENCOURAGEMENT

Rare is the business that doesn't experience occasional slumps. The business health of each of your customers is meaningful to you. In your travels you get a practical cross-section of business conditions. You know your clients and you can spot impending troubles with relative ease. In many cases the greatest service you can render to one or more customers is to give encouragement when it is needed.

Dear Perry,

From what you told me last time I saw you and from the recent reduction in your orders, I know how much the current slump must be worrying you.

Perry, this is a general situation. We see it happening all over the country. Nor is it new. Periods like this hit us every few years and they are hard to take. But I've never seen one that didn't end.

Right now there's every indication that the coming months will bring with them a great resurgence in sales. My company believes it to the extent that we are increasing inventories and are about to launch a powerful national advertising compaign.

My sincere advice, Perry, is to expect and to plan for unusually good business. Make a point of spreading that philosophy throughout your organization. If salesmen expect sales to be poor, they will be absolutely right. If they expect sales to be good, they'll be absolutely right. So much of selling success depends on the mental attitudes of the salesmen. We must recognize this and work to make them optimists . . . and right now optimism is justified.

I'll see you in three weeks and expect to find you glowing with good news.

Cordially,

Mark Your Calendar

All too often salesmen make the mistake of walking into a customer's offices unannounced. They know that they are expected within a few days, or a few weeks of the time they appear and assume that the buyer will be prepared to give them the time required. But this isn't always the case. The customer may be too busy to give the visiting salesman any time at all, in which case valuable selling time is lost. If your customer is busy, but tries to push some pressing matters aside to see and hear your presentation, the likelihood is that he will not give you as much time as he should and he may silently resent what he considers to be an inconsiderate intrusion.

Far better off is the salesman who writes ahead to state exactly when he will arrive, coupled with the request that his customer plan to spend time with him on a specific date and at a specific hour. Not only does such a request show appreciation for the buyer's time, but it demonstrates that the salesman places a value on his own time and on the importance of his reason for calling.

Dear Mr. Parkson,

I plan to be in your city throughout the week of May 21st.

Knowing how busy you are, I don't want to just walk in and disrupt your day. I have a number of new things to show you and some new ideas you'll find interesting. If it fits in with your schedule, may I have forty-five minutes with you starting at three in the afternoon on Tuesday, May 22nd?

If that is a suitable time for you, fine. I'll phone when I arrive to confirm it. If some other time would be better, I'll do my best to adjust my plans.

Sincerely,

Advance notice of a planned call carries even greater weight when you are fortified to pre-sell your reason for coming.

Dear Art,

When I call on you next month, I'll be bringing with me something really exciting. It is not something to buy. It's an idea that can give your sales a tremendous boost.

I picked up the idea on my travels. I've been adding some thoughts of my own to it and my conviction is that you are the man who can really make it pay off.

If you are sufficiently teased, let's plan on having dinner together Monday night, June 6th.

Cordially,

————————

Dear Bert,

I'm looking forward to my next visit to your city and the pleasure of seeing you again. I'll be there on September 9th.

In the meantime, if there is anything you need or anything I can do for you, just reach for the phone or write to me. If I'm out of town, my secretary knows how to handle anything you need.

Stay well and keep busy. See you next month.

Cordially,

———————

Dear Marty,

Line up the sales force for a meeting any evening during the second week of June.

I'll be there loaded with some great new sales approaches and some eye-opening new uses for our office copiers. If you want to make it a dinner meeting, go ahead and make the arrangements. I'll be delighted to play host.

Let me know if I can help in getting things organized.

My best . . .

In Summary . . . .

Don't trust to luck that even your friendliest customers will rebuff competing salesmen who happen to drop by at the strategic moment when inventories are low or services needed. A customer may be thoroughly aware of the fact that he can phone, write or wire your offices and ask for anything he wants; but when face-to-face with another salesman who is there to handle his needs, he is apt to take the easier course.

Use letters to represent you when you can't be present. You can put between-call letters to work to accomplish any of the following:

1. To fortify friendship and loyalty.
2. To take actions that show your interest and desire to serve.

3. To do favors that are not directly related to sales.
4. To offer needed encouragement.
5. To make it easier for customers to send you business between calls.
6. To pre-sell your reason for your next visit.
7. To arrange definite appointments for your next calls in a manner that will save your time and will win customer appreciation.

12

Letters to Send When a Prospect or Customer Was Unavailable

Every outside salesman knows the frustration of keeping an appointment only to find that the prospect or customer isn't there, or is too busy to be seen. Only slightly less disappointing is the unavailability of the people you call on without pre-arranged appointments.

More than wasted time is involved. When an appointment is broken there is the danger of your being irritated and letting it show. Revealing your anger or hurt feelings may give you momentary gratification, but it doesn't make sales.

When you fail to see somebody, a good letter can turn a loss into a potential profit. By the time you've found the time to write the letter, your temper, if it was aroused, has had time to cool off. You can then look at the circumstances more realistically and you often will realize that the breaking of the date may have been unavoidable. You can see, too, that you now have an advantage that you didn't have before.

Most people feel badly when they have to break a firm appointment. They feel guilty. A sense of obligation that didn't exist before may have been created. This is particularly true if you reveal your own thoughtfulness, consideration and understanding. Under such circumstances it becomes particularly easy for you to sell another appointment and, this time, you can be relatively certain that it will be kept.

BROKEN APPOINTMENTS

A gracious letter, revealing respect for the prospect and a continuing desire to serve . . . one that shows no resentment for an inconsiderate act . . . is likely to assure you unusual attention and a heightened desire to do business with you when the meeting finally takes place.

Dear Mr. Cattor,

Having heard so many interesting things about you, I had looked forward to our meeting. My disappointment, therefore, was twofold when I arrived for our appointment to learn that you were involved in a meeting.

The material I had prepared to review with you to clarify the key points in the insurance program we had discussed on the phone, will remain in my briefcase.

Your secretary has three choices of dates and hours for a new appointment and I will phone her tomorrow to learn which of them may fit in with your busy schedule.

Sincerely,

Your letter following a "no-show" appointment can also serve to increase the desire for your product or service.

Dear Mr. Markin,

Your secretary phoned this morning in time to cancel our visit to your offices. Thank you for sending word. I thoroughly understand how the unexpected can disrupt your scheduled activities.

Perhaps it was for the best.

Just before the cancellation we had been reviewing our planned presentation and our copy chief had a great new idea, but there wasn't time to capture it on paper and to permit our art department to portray its visual impact. Now we have the time and are hard at work on it. By tonight it will be ready.

I understand that you'll be back in the office Thursday and I'll phone to arrange another appointment.

Cordially,

————————

Dear Mr. Boosten,

When I reached your home at seven-thirty last night for our appointment, the house was dark and there was no answer to the door bell. Knowing your appreciation of the great importance of exploring ways and means of planning some method of financing the college educations of your children, I assumed that something of importance must have come up that made it impossible for you to be there.

Since time is so vital an ally when accumulating dollars, I suggest that we make another date at the earliest possible time.

I know that you don't like to be phoned at work so I will be grateful if you will phone me at 771-2458 to let me know when you and Mrs. Boosten would like me to come by. My secretary keeps my appointment schedules. If I am not in, she will be able to arrange a day and hour with you.

Cordially,

There are opportunities, when writing to people who didn't keep appointments, to stress the need for seeing you as soon as possible.

Dear Mrs. Mallory,

At ten-thirty this morning Mr. Jamison, one of our engineers, and I were at your home to keep our appointment with you. We waited for twenty minutes, but apparently something had come up that made it impossible for you to be there.

I know how much you and Mr. Mallory want your home air-conditioned before hot weather arrives.

Please call me at your first opportunity to make another appointment. This is our busy season and if we are to handle the installation, I'd like to get it scheduled as quickly as possible so that you won't be disappointed.

We have air-conditioned a number of homes in your neighborhood. Now that I have seen the exterior of your home I am confident that we can give you an estimate that will be a happy surprise for you.

Sincerely,

When illness is the reason for a broken date, there is that much more reason for you to show a considerate attitude.

Dear Mr. Collier,

I was extremely sorry to learn that you were home ill when I came to your plant yesterday for our meeting. By this time, I hope, you are feeling considerably better and will be able to return to your desk in the next day or two.

The chances are that a good deal of work will be waiting for your return, so I will not suggest another appointment until you have had time to catch up.

I'll phone one day next week to check with you.

Cordially,

Failure to See Your Party When You Just Drop In

There are many occasions when an advance appointment isn't possible or practical. Without an appointment you realize that your success in seeing your prospect or customer is a question of good luck and good timing. When you miss, your follow-through letter can set the stage for a future meeting when you'll be given an interested welcome.

Prospects who don't know you should be shown that they may have a substantial gain if they do meet you and hear your story. Your letter can give them the feeling that they have missed something by not being available when you called, providing motivation to make time to see you the next time you come by.

Dear Mr. Ellford,

I had hoped that I might find you with a few moments to spare when I called at your offices yesterday. Unhappily for me you were too busy at the time.

Mr. Ellford, I have seen several editions of your handsomely designed catalogues. My firm has just installed a new, high speed, high quality offset press that is ideally suited to your needs. I have an idea that would make future editions of your catalogues even more attractive and inviting to use. Our new equipment may also provide you with new economies.

May I have twenty minutes of your time to explore the possibilities with you? I'll phone before the week is out to ask for an appointment.

Sincerely,

———————

Dear Dr. Jollton,

You have one of the most attractive stores I've seen in a long time. I dropped in yesterday with the hope of meeting you, but I chose an unfortunate time. You were away for the day.

You, undoubtedly, are familiar with our nationally advertised cosmetics for men even though we've never had the good fortune of introducing our line to your store. Now that I have seen your store I'm certain that you could do extremely well with us.

My company has just devised one of the most compact and inviting display racks for our merchandise that the trade has seen. I found the very spot where it could be installed in your drug store, in a manner that will not replace or distract from any other display.

A week from Tuesday I'll be in your city again and I'm making a call on you my number one mission.

I look forward to meeting you.

Sincerely,

———————

Dear Mr. Lockway,

Yesterday afternoon I pulled up in front of your plant in a gleaming new truck. I was there to invite you to see-for-yourself the wonderful new features introduced for the first time in this year's models.

You were out at that time and I was sorry to miss you, but it is such a pleasure to drive our new trucks I'm more than glad to drive back.

Mr. Lockway, I've studied the fleet you now use. You have certain special requirements. You need a compact panel truck that can carry a good pay-load . . . you need ruggedness . . . you need safety and you need economy of operation. You also need a fleet the represents you well wherever one of your trucks is seen.

That's why I look forward to driving back. You'll want to see the way our new panel trucks fit every one of those requirements so handsomely.

Would Monday morning at ten be a good time for you? I'll phone at the end of the week to ask that question. I hope that I've made a happy choice for you.

Cordially,

If the prospect's office is out of town and you are not likely to return to his city for the foreseeable future, it is important that you suggest a means of taking action easily.

Dear Mr. Groover,

While I was in your city on Tuesday of this week, I called on you but, unfortunately, you were out of town.

Your secretary, who was most courteous, accepted several copies of our publication and our rate card. I hope you've found the time to review them.

Enclosed is a detailed break-down of our subscribers. This is fresh material, the result of a survey completed only recently.

Our magazine reaches the kind of people who are your best prospects. It strikes me as a natural for your advertising and I'm convinced that your use of our pages will pay handsome dividends for you.

I'm always at my desk on Thursdays and Fridays. Please call me collect if I can give you any additional information and assistance.

Sincerely,

A touch of light humor, linked to the lure of profit, will serve you well in many cases. The light touch makes you a more desirable person to meet.

Dear Mr. Copplin,

I miss you.

That may sound strange, coming from someone you've never met. But it is true.

I cover your city the first week of each month. Until yesterday I had missed the fact that you had opened a sporting goods store. When I dropped in yesterday afternoon you had just left for the day. I certainly have missed you.

What a handsome store you have.

Please, Mr. Copplin, reserve some time for me around ten in the morning on October 9th. That's when I'll be back, and I'm determined not to miss you again . . . determined that you should no longer miss the profit opportunities our line of sporting equipment can bring you.

Sincerely,

Regular calls on steady customers in your own town seldom require appointments. Here too, however, you often will call at an inopportune time and be unable to see your customer. If the purpose of the call was to introduce a new item or a new idea that you feel will be particularly interesting to your account, a letter can help you to dramatize the importance of the call and the desirability of seeing you at the first opportunity.

Dear Harry,

Sorry I missed you when I dropped in yesterday.

We just took on a new line of fine printing papers, and I left a portfolio of samples with Mike. He said he would show them to you. Take a few moments to look them over, Harry. I think you'll be fascinated with some of the great colors these people make available. The printing quality is excellent.

I'll give you a ring in the next day or two to see if you'd like to have some dummy sheets for presentations to some of your customers. If you'd like me to come by to discuss the use of these or any of our other papers, just say the word and I'll be delighted to make a date with you.

My best . . .

———————

Dear Miss Glenn,

I'm a bad picker. I picked yesterday afternoon to drop by to show you an ingenious new filing system we now carry. I picked a time when you were in a meeting.

You'll want to see this because it offers a solution to a problem you've mentioned to me several times. As soon as I saw it, I thought of your need and . . . that's when I did the bad picking . . . hurried right over.

How about Friday morning, around ten?

If that's a bad time for you, please give me a ring; otherwise I'll be there.

                                        Cordially,

In Summary . . . .

When people don't keep appointments or aren't available when you visit them without appointments, you can turn your loss to a profit through the use of letters. Your letters can:

1. Add to the sense of obligation.
2. Help to pre-sell.
3. Build the realization that time is important.
4. Demonstrate your thoughtfulness.
5. Motivate prospects to want to see you.
6. Stress value and service.
7. Make good customers want to see you right away.

13

Letters Covering Complaints

Write long letters. That is rare advice concerning business letters. When it comes to answers to complaints, however, it is usually sound advice. Most replies to complaints call for detailed explanations. The more detailed the explanation the more you are revealing your genuine interest in the complaint. Nobody likes to have his complaint brushed aside or handled lightly.

People don't like to be complainers. There are exceptions, of course, but the average individual enjoys being regarded as fair, generous and a good fellow. To complain by-passes those pleasant images. In almost all cases, therefore, no matter how much a complaint may annoy you, or appear unreasonable, you can be relatively certain that the customer felt he was completely justified in sounding off.

UNREASONABLE COMPLAINTS

One of the most difficult letters of this type is the really unreasonable complaint. Everyone in business gets them from time-to-time. Often they come from good customers. It isn't good business to bow to an unjustified, unreasonable complaint, for, in doing so, you are opening the door to others. The big problem with the reply you write is that you must find a way to convincingly show that the complaint is not justified, without inflicting wounds on the customer's pride or reflecting on his intelligence. You are faced with the task of telling the customer that he is wrong, while trying to hold his good will for future business.

115

Dear Mr. Poole,

Your telling me to cancel all of your policies because your recent claim was refused concerns me deeply. It concerns me for a number of reasons and the foremost is that you will be hurting yourself.

Mr. Poole, I thoroughly understand your disappointment that the company didn't pay the claim. Insurance has many complicated, technical aspects and unless one is trained in such matters it isn't easy to understand the refusal of what appears to be a legitimate request for payment.

The policy in question covers you for liability for any damage you may do to people or property while driving your car. You were legally responsible for damages to Mr. Downs' car when you released his brake and pushed his car forward in order to get your own car out of a parking space. The company's attorneys have taken the position that you were not in your own car at the time and, therefore, were not covered by the terms of your policy. Similar cases have been in the courts, and the company's decision is amply supported by precedent.

As your agent I promptly filed your claim and did my best to try to get payment for you. An agent doesn't make the final decisions.

Were you to cancel all of your policies because of this, replacing them, which is most important to you, would add to your premium expense. This is especially true of your life policies. And I'm sure you realize, too, that the company that turned down your automobile damage claim has nothing to do with most of your other insurance protection.

I have written this letter so that you may have the opportunity to review and to consider the facts involved before making a firm decision. On Friday I will call on you with the hope that you have reconsidered. Please do, for you will be adding damage on top of damage if you do not.

Sincerely,

———————————

Dear Mrs. Pallage,

Your unhappiness at the loss you experienced when you sold your XYZ stock is understandable. I share your unhappiness.

Your letter, as you can imagine, disturbed me. You have taken me to task because of your loss, but let us review what happened.

In October you asked my advice regarding an investment in a good oil stock. I went over the report of our research department with you and suggested XYZ because it appeared to offer reasonable income and long-term growth possibilities. These are the elements you want and need. The decision was made to buy 200 shares.

In February, during a period of generally declining stock prices, you phoned and expressed concern over your XYZ stock. I explained that our research people still thought highly of it and that you should be patient; that the dividends were unaffected by the fluctuations in the price of the stock and I was confident that, in time, the price would reach its former levels and could go beyond them. Despite that you sold your shares.

You did incur a loss, which was regrettable. The sale that realized the loss was contrary to my thinking and suggestions. Certainly, my advice that you hold, and do not sell, could not be regarded as self-serving. My income is created through the commissions earned when my customers buy or sell, not when they hold.

Since your sale, XYZ stock has regained its former price position and has even risen two points.

I enjoy working with you, Mrs. Pallage, and hope you'll continue to have confidence in my desire to help you. I cannot and do not expect you to accept all of my suggestions and by no means do I hold myself forth as infallible . . . far from it. If we are to continue what had been a most harmonious relationship, however, I do feel that there must be mutual trust and understanding.

Your letter, I am sure, was written impulsively. On reviewing the facts, I'm equally sure that you will appreciate that nothing I said or did justifies your displeasure with me. Don't you agree?

My sincere regards and good wishes.

Sincerely,

You Have to Say "No"

Next in line, in terms of difficulty, is the customer that complains about something your company does or doesn't do. The customer wants a change made, but it can't or won't be done.

The first thing to look for before you begin to compose your letter, is a reason for refusal *from the customer's point of view*. You won't always find it, but you will, if you try, in a surprising number of cases.

A second point of importance when saying "no" in such cases, is to show that the request has been given great consideration. Never hang your refusal on the puny word, "policy." *"We are sorry, but what you ask for is contrary to company policy."* That explains nothing. Your customer couldn't care less about company policy. Policies can be changed. Tell him precisely why the company has decided that they must operate in a certain manner. The likelihood is that the firm you work for has mighty good reasons for doing things the way they do and it is your job to reveal those reasons in understandable detail. Businessmen . . . people in general . . . understand that your company has to make profits and must have uniform practices. Give your complainers the opportunity to see these elements clearly and they can accept the negative decisions.

Dear Will,

That is a really interesting idea you've presented.

I took your letter to our production manager, and he has given it a lot of consideration.

His conclusion, I'm sorry to say, is that it wouldn't be practical for us to make the change. While the innovation is particularly suitable for your area, it would not meet with approval in other parts of the country.

True, we could make a special run embracing your idea for you and, perhaps, for a few others who might welcome the idea, but we have been able to mass produce and hold our prices down because we do not deviate. Special production for a small number of outlets would require that we charge you more per unit which would hurt your own competitive position.

I wish we could handle your request, Will, but it looks as though it would not be good for you or for us.

My warmest regards.

Cordially,

————————

Dear Al,

You're right, Al, many manufacturers do have co-op advertising programs with their outlets. I can certainly see merit in the idea.

The boss and I both read your letter and we had the advertising manager in, too.

Even though the company has had a policy against co-op advertising for as many years as I have been in the company, your letter occasioned a whole review of the stand we've taken. You can take that as a compliment, since it was your name that inspired this reconsideration session.

The final conclusion, however, was that no change should be made, and I'm convinced that this is good from your viewpoint, as well as our own.

As you know, we believe in advertising. That is well demonstrated by our national magazine, radio and television campaigns. Were we to also budget for co-op advertising in each city where we have outlets, a sizeable sum would have to be taken out of the national effort. The conviction is that this, in time, would make our line less known, would reduce demand and you, along with other retailers, would feel the difference in reduced sales.

In national advertising, we have complete control and we dominate with our full page ads and our broadcasts. Co-op ads generally are parts of larger ads covering many items, and the impact is considerably less.

Count on us, Al, for total cooperation on special displays, statement stuffers and my personal cooperation. These are always yours for the asking. On the co-op ads, however, I hope you'll see that, in the long run, you are better served if we continue to put all the dollars we can into backing you up with our national effort.

See you soon.

Cordially,

BILLING AND CREDIT COMPLAINTS

A high percentage of complaints are prompted by misunderstandings about prices or over-taxing of credit. These are delicate subjects that call for delicate handling. This is particularly true where credit curtailment is involved.

Don't make the mistake of joining sides with your customer against the company. The easy letter to write is to call the credit manager dirty names or to condemn the company's practices. Dodging the issue in such a manner may retain your image as one of the "good guys" but it does nothing to help you to hold the complainer's business. You've gone on record as representing "bad guys," which hardly inspires people to give your company future business *despite you*.

Here, too, you frequently can look for and find reasons that represent the customer's point of view.

Dear Mr. Barrot,

I can fully understand your unhappiness with the letter you received from Mr. Kraal, our credit manager. You have been a good customer of ours for a number of years, and his refusal to grant further credit at this time was naturally upsetting.

When the decision was made, I had a long talk with Joe Kraal. He, too, was unhappy about the situation, as was reflected in his letter. In expressing his feelings to me, he said that his rejection of further credit at this time was for your benefit as well as the company's. Payments for past purchases are four months in arrears and, he pointed out, a further extension of credit would magnify your problems.

Your city has been hard hit by that strike that has had so many people out of work for a long time. When the strike is settled your sales, unquestionably, will come back to normal and even reach new heights. Until that happens, however, you are beset by sales and collection problems. Looking at your problem as a credit man . . . and he's a good one . . . Joe Kraal is convinced that your best course is to hold back on purchasing and all other expenditures until you have weathered the storm.

Understanding the problems you now face, he is entirely willing to give you ample time to clear up your present indebtedness with us. As soon as your business is back to normal, I'm sure our relationship will follow suit.

My sincerest good wishes for a quick recovery.

Cordially,

———————

Dear Mr. Monrow,

When your letter pointing out what appeared to be an error in our invoice, reached my desk today, I immediately pulled the file with our correspondence.

You are right when you say that I quoted you a lower price, but if you'll review our exchange of letters, as I have done, you'll see that the price

quoted was based on your original inquiry about 400 cartons. You sub-
sequently sent us a purchase order for 250 cartons. That is why the price
I quoted and the one on your invoice don't agree.

The letter specifying the price for 400 stated that there was a price-break
at 350. To save you the trouble of going through your own files, I am
enclosing our carbon of the letter.

This, I hope, clarifies the question. Thank you for giving me the opportunity to do so.

Cordially,

Dear Mr. Ingalos,

For many years our company has handled all shipments on an FOB our
plant basis. This has been our practice because we have uniform prices
in our catalogs and did not feel we could include shipping costs since
it would penalize our many customers in and around the city of origin.

With this letter I am giving you another copy of the catalog from which
you ordered. You'll see that all prices show, "FOB our Plant."

When you placed your order, you undoubtedly concentrated on the item
description and the price and overlooked the FOB notice. I'm truly sorry
that the shipping charge was unexpected in your case.

Again, many thanks for your order. I hope you'll get great value from the
equipment you ordered. I look forward to seeing you on my next trip.

Cordially,

SOMEONE ELSE AT FAULT

Watch this type of reply to a complaint carefully. It is much too easy
to joyfully write a letter saying, "You're blaming the wrong man," when
an investigation of a complaint proves that somebody else is the villain
in the piece. In the first place, you are involved to some degree since the
complaint is connected with your product or service. Secondly, you can
create an extremely poor impression if you simply pass the buck and fail
to evidence genuine concern about an error. Thirdly, you are on very
thin ice if you point the finger, no matter how accurately, at the cus-

tomer himself or one of his employees. Finally, you may be passing up an opportunity to demonstrate the depth of your interest in a customer and his problems if you don't involve yourself in the adjustment.

When you respond to complaints that may be attributed to others, be sure to put yourself in the picture. Tell what you are doing or have done to help correct the situation, even though another is responsible.

Dear Mr. Henry,

I completely understand your anger and your disappointment. When you phoned me Thursday morning, an hour before your audience was due, to tell me that the film hadn't arrived, I felt physically ill. I could clearly visualize your predicament.

The whole episode has been thoroughly investigated. Your order for the film reached us on the afternoon of the eighteenth. The film was checked out and was taken to the airport before eleven on the morning of the nineteenth. It should have been in your airport that evening and in your hands the morning of the twentieth. With your show scheduled for Thursday, the twenty-second, we were confident that there would be no problem.

Both we and the airline are still checking. Seemingly, the film must have been put on the wrong flight or wasn't taken off when it reached your airport. It is still missing.

Enclosed is a photo copy of the bill of lading. It was a relief to see that we had addressed the film properly, and the bill of lading confirms the date and hour when it was turned over to the airline.

Although the error was not in our offices, and beyond our control, I sincerely apologize for the occurrence. Knowing your ingenuity, I'm certain that you improvised in a manner that saved the day and I hope that, despite everything, the meeting was productive.

When we eventually get an answer to the mysterious disappearance, I'll give you the facts.

Cordially,

———————

Dear Owen,

Please destroy the catalogs. We've gone back to press.

You are going to lose ten days getting in the mail, but your catalog will be right. What a heart break after all the thought, time and effort that went into the production. But this is the handsomest book you've ever produced and, in my judgment, the delay won't take away from the eventual results.

Tom Mally, the production manager of Arclight Bindery, met with me yesterday afternoon just after the fiasco had been discovered. The two of us went over the signatures as they had come off our presses, and he agrees that they were properly planned. The mistake was made in the folding and the collation in his plant. We had provided them with a hand-folded and properly collated and trimmed dummy, but the error happened all the same.

Fortunately, there is no need to remake negatives and plates, so no time has been lost in going back to press.

Since Mally accepts the responsibility, I presume that there will be no problem about Arclight's acceptance of the cost of the rerun. But knowing the urgency of your need, I ordered the rerun immediately and didn't delay it until we had an understanding with them. This is their problem and our problem, not yours.

My great regrets, Owen. You can be sure that we'll do our utmost to cut hours and days off the production time and will send one of our men to Arclight with the completed job to be certain that the error is not repeated.

Cordially,

––––––––––

Dear Mr. Gammon,

This morning after receiving your letter, I phoned Harry Merks in your accounting division. I have good news for you.

When the machine wouldn't perform as I had promised, I can understand your being unhappy. I suspected what the trouble might be and, after talking with Mr. Merks for a few minutes, my hunch proved to be right.

When the machine was assembled in your office one unit was put in backwards. While I held the phone, Mr. Merks corrected that and came right back to the phone to tell me that all was well.

By now you undoubtedly have heard about it from him and know that the machine is doing everything it is supposed to do.

And we are indebted to you.

The error was a natural one. We are at fault, not your people. The part that went in wrong seems to fit properly in either position, but only works when in the right position. From now on we are going to stencil that trouble-maker with explicit instructions.

Please forgive us for not being more precise in our instructions, but I am relieved and happy that the problem was so easily and quickly adjusted.

Sincerely,

You Are Guilty

If you were wrong, say so, and say it at once. Don't try to cover the error under a pile of words. We are quick to forgive the man who says, "You are right . . . I was wrong," but we'll resent the man who tries to hide his error and dodge the responsibility.

Errors that can be corrected by compensatory action may cease to be viewed as errors provided that action is taken with speed and without red tape. If you plan to compensate, therefore, reveal that intention in the opening of your letter.

Dear Mr. Horrace,

A new, and correct, shipment was rushed to you by air this morning.

Your telegram shook me up considerably and for the next hour I had everyone here well shaken too. The folks in our shipping department are pretty much on the ball, but when they pull a boner they do it well.

I can't tell you how sorry all of us are. We know how much you were counting on having that merchandise in time for the opening of your branch store and all we gave you was a problem.

I now have my fingers crossed that no further errors, bad weather or anything else delays the new shipment. It may still reach you in time and I'll phone tomorrow hoping you'll tell me that it did . . . and that all is forgiven.

At your own convenience, please have the wrong consignment shipped back to us collect.

The best to you on the opening.

Cordially,

———————

Dear Paul,

You are right and the magazine is right . . . we missed the deadline.

Telling you how sorry I am doesn't alter the facts. It doesn't put your message before the public during the week when your heavy air time is scheduled. Our traffic people mis-read a date and, what is more important, I failed to follow through. I should have.

This morning I phoned the magazine. They feel as badly about it as I do even though they were not at fault. The plate is now in their hands, and I've been promised the best position in the book . . . page three . . . for the next edition. There's some consolation in that but it doesn't make up for my failure to check.

Next week I'll be in to offer my apologies in person. Please beat me. I deserve it.

Cordially,

———————

Dear Joe,

This morning we went back to press and will work around the clock to re-print your job . . . correctly.

The fault was entirely ours. We triple-goofed.

As soon as I learned about the error I dug out your okay'd proofs. You couldn't have marked the correction more clearly. It was overlooked by the composing room . . . overlooked by the foreman . . . overlooked by me. And, as we all know far too well, the entire press run carried the original boner.

When something like this happens, you can theorize and philosophize endlessly about how three people could be guilty of the same crime but that doesn't excuse or correct the harm done.

I have one happy note to add.

When you and I first discussed the job, you were anxious to use that handsome, special finish offset stock I showed you, but reluctantly turned it down because of the extra cost involved. The rerun will be on that better stock and the difference will be absorbed by us. I hope that this, to some degree, will help to compensate for the time lost.

Thanks for your understanding and patience, Joe. I apologize for all of us and you can be sure that the whole plant will be standing a little higher on their toes from now on.

Cordially,

In Summary . . . .

Don't hold back when writing letters responding to complaints. The customer who complains feels a great sense of justification and is entitled to a detailed reply. Your answer to a complaint, justified or not, can strengthen your relationship with a customer if you handle it with thoughtful care.

1. Write long letters of explanation.
2. Don't give-in to unreasonable requests.
3. Save your customer's pride.
4. Explain refusals from his point of view.
5. Don't hide behind the word "policy."
6. Show that great consideration was given.
7. Don't blame it on the company.
8. Step carefully when another is at fault.
9. Involve yourself in corrective steps even though another is to blame.
10. If you are wrong, say so fast.
11. If corrective action is taken, announce it at once.

14

Effective Uses of Unusual Letter Styles

Over the years, business letters have become severely stylized. Nearly all of the letters in the preceding chapters, and those to follow, have adhered to some extent, to the physical form that one expects. They start with the formal salutation, "Dear So-and-So," several paragraphs follow and then there is the complimentary close and signature.

But it doesn't have to be done that way.

Just as imaginative, personable salesmen distinguish themselves by taking fresh approaches in their contacts with customers and prospects, so many letters written by salesmen have freshness and differences that catch the eye and hold the attention.

"Way-Out" letters are not for everybody. The highly conservative, quiet salesman might be taking the wrong path were he to use letters that were sharply in conflict with his own personality. But most salesmen will see in the letters that follow some departures from the standard letter form that will help them to reflect their own images effectively . . . that will enable them to make their correspondence more interesting and compelling, and better remembered.

Before electing to use a "Way-Out" letter, however, consider not only your own personality, but the personality of the intended reader. If the man you are writing to is a stickler for the sedate and the conservative, your departure from the familiar may shock and repel him. But if he is an imaginative, progressive innovator himself, you can be certain that the novel letter will intrigue him and will build your image in his eyes.

127

NOVEL TO SEE AS WELL AS TO READ

First, let's consider some "Way-Out" letters that proclaim their originality by the way they look.

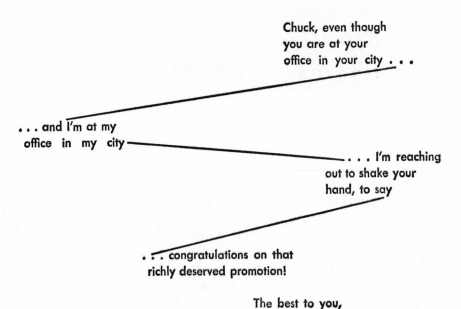

The best to you,

———————

MR. BENSON . . .

thanks is a small word for that

BIG ORDER.

But my

THANKS

are BIG.

Gratefully,

Wonderful news, Mr. Grace
the market is .

. . . . (vertical dots)

     down . . .

You've been investing $100 every month in your mutual fund accumulation program. Right now securities' values have taken a sharp drop. To some extent your fund's shares must follow the market . . . and that's great.

This month, for example, your $100 will buy 12 new shares for your account, while last month the same $100 bought only 9 and a fraction shares.

The history of the securities market has been that every market dip has been followed by new highs, if given enough time. This is bargain-buying time.

You have good reason to rejoice in occasional market slumps because you have a good many years to go before you complete your share accumulation program.

                                  Cordially,

The third of the above letters is considerably more subdued than the others. Properly so. It discusses a serious subject. At the same time the writer was determined to lure Mr. Grace into attentive reading, and the opening of the letter almost guarantees total attention.

WHAT YOU SAY . . . NOT JUST HOW IT'S TYPED

A "Way-Out" letter goes well beyond looking different. The use of this no-holds-barred manner of communicating primarily embraces how you express yourself. It often is a sound idea to literally jar people into accepting a point of view. In many lines of business the writing of a letter of estimate is a frequent necessity, but it usually becomes an exceptionally formal letter, even when written to a customer who has become a close, personal friend. But that isn't necessary.

Thank you, Joe . . .

You asked for an estimate on 75,000 four-color folders . . .

The estimate is—*nothing*.

Eventually, of course, you'd get our bill for $2,780, but this is *nothing* compared with the pride you'll take in the quality of the completed folders . . . in the impact they will have when you put them to work . . . in the peace of mind you will have knowing that the work is in the hands of the most skillful and most reliable printers in the area.

I'll see you at ten, Monday morning, to ask when we can start production.

My best . . .

Humor Has Its Place

Everyone enjoys being amused and when you manage to make a customer smile, you've made a better friend. Humor must be handled with caution. If it is inappropriate, off-color, too bold or too subtle, it can backfire. But the light humor embodied in this next letter from a men's clothing salesman to customers he knows well can be unusually resultful.

Dear Mr. Perce,

Please be sure that somebody is at your home at two in the afternoon this coming Tuesday.

I have told the Salvation Army to come there at that time to pick up all of your fall and winter suits.

Cordially,

P.S. I almost forgot to mention that I did that for you because when you see the outstanding new cloths, colors and styles of this year's offerings you won't want to wear anything else. They are here to see right now.

P.P.S. Be sure to let me know that somebody will be home for the Salvation Army truck because they won't come by without confirmation.

A degree of humor is also a useful tool when you must confess to an error, particularly if you make yourself the butt of the joke.

Mr. Horace, you are
cordially invited to
a public lynching . . .

My request that I be hung from the highest tree in town has been granted.

I made the request when I learned that I had been guilty of shipping the wrong merchandise. A correct shipment is on its way.

Please return the first case, express collect, and don't miss being an official witness of my execution.

I am embarrassed and deeply apologetic for my boner. I hope it didn't cause you undue trouble.

Cordially,

One warning . . . don't employ humor when writing about an error that is taken very seriously by the customer. If he has been badly inconvenienced or has lost money because of a mistake, he won't appreciate your thinking that the incident is funny.

Unnecessary Letters

The unnecessary letter . . . one that doesn't attempt to sell, inform, adjust or anything else . . . but simply transmits a genuine expression of appreciation . . . particularly lends itself to unique treatment.

This is a "nothing" letter, Al . . .

It brings you nothing in the way of news or announcements.

It has nothing to do with business.

It is simply to say that there is nothing I cherish more than some of the wonderful friendships I have formed over the years, and would take nothing in place of the warm and delightful relationship I have enjoyed in working with you.

I had nothing else in mind.

Nothing but the best to you . . .

THE NEW CUSTOMER

You've just landed a new account and made your first sale to him. Now you want to say thanks in a manner that will make him glad he did business with you and anxious to do more. Here, again, is a particularly appropriate time to demonstrate your imagination and your sincerity.

You did a great
selling job, Mr. Wence . . .

No, I don't have that backwards. True, you bought some merchandise from me, but I came away from our session completely sold on you and what you are doing.

You sold me on the desire to apply all the thought and effort and energy I possess to make my firm, its products and services vital to you.

My warmest thanks for your initial order. I'll be back to see you soon and I eagerly look forward to it.

Cordially,

THE PROSPECT YOU DIDN'T SELL

Although you didn't make a sale on your first call to a new prospect, you see great potential. You want to impress your name and image on the prospect's mind in a manner that will oil the hinges on his door the next time you call on him.

Mr. Phelps, you pitched
a no hit game yesterday . . .

I came up to bat in your office hoping to get on base, but I struck out.

But I enjoyed the game.

Next season I hope that my timing will be better . . . that I'll become a player on *your* team.

Thanks for giving me my turn at bat.

Cordially,

The Prospect Who Responded to an Ad

People who mail in coupons or reply cards asking for a demonstration can be further pre-sold . . . pre-sold on you as well as the product. Your use of a letter with sparkle can motivate the prospect to happily anticipate your call, simply because you sound like someone who'll be pleasant to meet.

I'll be there, Mr. Ruth . . .

Thanks for sending in the card asking for a demonstration of our new dry copier at three next Thursday.

You'll see much more than an advanced process in photo copying . . . you'll see new speed, new efficiencies, new ease of handling and new economies.

I look forward to meeting you.

Sincerely,

The Prospect You Hope to See

The light and personable touch can be immensely more rewarding than a customary, formal letter approach. You not only want to get an appointment with the potential customer, you want to be received with happy anticipation.

This is a warning, Mr. Caulley . . .

For a long time I've been hearing many fine things about your store . . . your merchandising skills . . . your fine reputation as an individual.

And I've made up my mind, Mr. Caulley, that I not only want to meet you, but that the meeting will mark the start of a long and mutually rewarding relationship.

I hope that you have heard some good things about my firm. But it doesn't matter. When we meet, you will.

On November 10th I arrive in your city and I'll phone to ask if I may have an appointment.

Don't say I didn't warn you.

Sincerely,

ADVANCE EXCITEMENT ABOUT NEW MERCHANDISE

If you are excited about the qualities of a new line or some new service you are about to offer, transmit it by making your letter as exciting as your news. Start the fire burning before you arrive on the scene. Don't go overboard, however, for if you light a torch and can back it up with no more than a spark, you'll burn down your welcome. If excitement is fully justified, be excited. If it isn't, keep your fire cool.

You may never see
me again, Pete . . .

I'm writing this during my seventh orbit of the moon.

Yesterday the firm had the entire sales force together for the unveiling of our new fall line.

Pete, you know all the whispering and hinting we've been hearing about the new designers . . . the new fabrics . . . the new colors. My hopes were high, but when I saw what we have I zoomed past my highest hopes, went into orbit and have yet to re-enter.

You'll be joining me in outer space the moment I can get my samples and hop on a plane.

Cordially,

WHEN A CUSTOMER IS ILL

When you get the word that a customer is on the sick list you, naturally, want to convey your hopes for a complete and rapid recovery.

Use caution. If the man is seriously ill and there is concern about the future, don't try to be frivolous. If the condition is not serious, however, there are few things you can do that will be better appreciated than to send a letter calculated to evoke a chuckle or a smile.

Otto, when a buyer
buys a bed in a
hospital . . . that's ridiculous . . .

The news just reached me today. At first I was worried, but then I thought about it.

I recall that I wasn't feeling so hot some time ago and I went to the doctor. I said "Doc, I'm a big boy. Pull no punches. Tell me in plain language, what's wrong with me?"

He said, "Okay, I'll make it clear. You're lazy."

So I said, "Fine, Doc, now tell me what it is in fancy terms, so I can tell my boss."

Now, I'm not accusing you of being lazy, or of using your hospitalization insurance to steal some solid rest and relaxation.

But I'm suspicious.

To allay my suspicions, Otto . . . get out of there fast and get back to work.

The best to you, Otto . . .

Sales Manager Can Use "Way-Out" Letters Too

Of the many letters a sales manager must write to his men in the field, the congratulatory and the pep letters are the ones most likly to get heavy and sound insincere. Going "Way-Out" can help to overcome those problems.

Congratulations, Mel . . .

You just made a hole in one!

It's a fact. You just made a hole in the company's sales records.

Your sales for the past month will be a ringing challenge to every other pro who tries to play the course.

But I'm betting, Mel, that the next man to break the record will be . . . Mel.

Cheers . . .

————————

You're off your rocker, Harry . . .

. . . and I'm delighted.

For a long time both you and I were concerned because you'd been in the doldrums . . . your customary zip and energy were AWOL.

But this month's sales report makes it wonderfully evident that you are out of the rocking chair and back on your horse.

I couldn't be happier, Harry and I know that you, too, must be bursting with pleasure.

Keep going.

My best . . .

In Summary . . . .

"Way-Out" letters, if they fit your personality and the personality of the reader, can build your image, will be appreciated and remembered, if you . . .

1. Use a physical form that commands attention.
2. Express yourself in imaginative terms.
3. Employ humor that is appropriate and in good taste.
4. Transmit a message of sincere appreciation to a customer.
5. Impress a new customer with your desire to serve.
6. Pave the way for a call-back on a prospect who didn't buy.
7. Build anticipation with a prospect who asked you to call.
8. Seek an appointment with a new prospect.
9. Create advance excitement about new merchandise.
10. Cheer an ailing customer.
11. As a sales manager, want to convey genuine praise.

15

Sales Ideas for Men in the Field

Chapters 15 through 19 are primarily for the Sales Manager, but should be helpful to the Salesman, too. Letters included deal with a wide variety of situations, and each is designed to promote confidence and communication between the manager and his salesmen.

When writing to your salesmen, in the effort to put across an idea, you have to apply yourself to doing a selling job every bit as much as when trying to make a point by mail with a customer.

If you have a sound idea to pass along to the men in the field . . . an idea calculated to increase sales . . . surely it is worth the extra effort and cost that will assure maximum adoption. If it isn't read, or is read quickly and casually, you can't expect maximum adoption.

One of the more important of your duties as a sales manager is the need to supply your salesmen with a constant flow of compelling and practical new sales ideas. You are in an ideal situation to be able to carry out this responsibility. Your continuing contact with your salesmen enables you to learn of a variety of novel approaches individual men have tried, tested and proven. Trade publications frequently report on new ideas and new trends in selling. Business meetings, conventions and trade shows put you in touch with others in the same or similar fields and provide the opportunity to hear of new techniques.

When writing to your salesmen to transmit new ideas, don't take it for granted that because they work for you they necessarily will read anything you write with total interest and attention.

A great number of sales ideas are reduced to mimeographed or photo-offset bulletins. From a production standpoint this is the most economical method of transmitting information. But from a practical standpoint it may prove to be the most costly method. A mass produced bulletin says, by its physical nature, "I'm for everybody." An individually typed letter says, "This is a personal message to you." Obviously, the latter is the one that will get the greatest attention.

Idea for a Printing Salesman

Here's an idea for printing salesmen that addresses itself to their greatest interest from the start ... making more money ... and hands them precise language to use and an action they can take.

Dear Frank,

Here's a money-maker for you.

We've all had our full share of meeting with prospects who seem impressed with our facilities and service story . . . who make vague promises . . . and nothing happens.

In many cases those people half-way mean what they say. At that moment they are leaning toward you. The big problem, as you know, is that they usually don't have a printing job ready to hand over that day. At that moment in time there is no sale to close. And . . . what happens? A few days or a few weeks later, when there is a job to hand out, the impression you made has been diluted by dozens of other things that have demanded his attention and he reverts to habit . . . he calls his old printer. That's the easiest thing for him to do.

Try this . . .

From now on, when you wind up a well accepted presentation, and there is no job to be quoted or carried home at the moment, ask, "Are there any days of the week or times of the month when you generally have printing to be done?"

Experience has shown that a good percentage of our customers . . . and it follows that this probably is true of prospects too . . . have precise dates when printing requirements reach the ready line. Newsletters, service mailings, reports, etc., often are readied for printing Thursdays and Fridays. Some firms take inventory of printed forms at the end of each month . . . and so on.

If your prospect says, "Most of our printing is given out around the first of each month," . . . great!

You say, "Mr. Prospect, as a help to you I'm going to make a practice of dropping by to see you the first of each month from now on. You won't have to bother calling me." Maybe . . . depending on where your prospect is located, or how many others you have to peg for the same day . . . you may say that you'll phone. In either case you are taking the action on your own shoulders and not depending on his memory or motivation.

Put the idea to work, Frank. You'll find that it is well received, it licks one of the most persistent problems you have, and will make money for you.

Cordially,

IDEA FOR A MUTUAL FUND SALESMAN

Don't just explain an idea. Bring it to life with a believable example demonstrating how it can be applied, as is done in this letter.

Dear Pete,

Imagine with me for a moment . . . for I think you'll see some extra commissions in your future if you will.

You've just finished a complete mutual fund presentation to a young couple in their home. They have a six-year-old son and they have told you that they definitely want their boy to have a college education. Right now they have no plan to finance that education and you've shown them how an accumulation program may fit their needs. But they won't make up their minds. The session is about to end. You are going to leave there empty handed and they will be no better off then than they were when you arrived.

Before you leave . . . *disturb them.*

Pick up your briefcase and stand up. Say just two words, "I apologize."

Now they are confused and puzzled. You have spent an hour or two of your time explaining and offering help. They probably feel a bit guilty that they are sending you on your way with nothing for your efforts. And here you are apologizing to *them.* One of them is bound to ask WHY?

"You've shown me that you have a serious financial need. When your boy is ready for college somebody is going to pay for it . . you, because you've prepared . . . or your son, because you haven't prepared. He'll pay for it the rest of his life if he can't have a higher education. Somehow, I failed to impress you with the great importance of taking action now. I've let you and your son down and . . . I apologize."

Either of two things is likely to happen.

They'll ask you to sit down again and they will make a decision to start now . . . or, because you left them disturbed and unhappy, you'll get a phone call in a day or so asking you to return.

College . . . retirement . . . income now . . . it doesn't matter what the objective is, you always can leave prospects disturbed. With your training you are better aware of financial needs than the people you approach. You have an obligation to them to jar them into full appreciation of their needs.

Use this idea, Pete. It will help our prospects and it will help you.

Cordially,

IDEA FOR A LIFE INSURANCE SALESMAN

Notice the final line in the letter that follows. You ask the salesman to report on what happens when he tries the idea out. Reading that request, he knows that you haven't just offered an offhand suggestion. You have given him a new selling tool to put to work and you expect to have a report on its effectiveness. This is a simple means of adding another bit of motivation to use the ideas you generate.

Dear Mac,

There are many ways to close a life insurance sale.

I'm dropping you this line to give you one that can pay off handsomely.

First, let's see if we agree on two facts:

1. Most men don't like to think about dying prematurely.

2. Most men like to show their wives and children that they love them.

Are we agreed?

Okay. The next time you wind-up a presentation on a life contract, try this:

"Mr. Prospect, whenever family occasions come along you, undoubtedly, are generous and thoughtful in your gift giving. It is one way of showing your wife and children how deeply you love them. Is that right?

"You'll seldom have as fine an opportunity to demonstrate to your family how much they mean to you than you have right now. When you sign this application, you can go home tonight and tell your wife and children the step you have taken to be certain that, no matter what happens, you have seen to it that they can live without problems or sacrifices. You'll be giving them a gift of comfort and security."

Not only does that close shift the prospect's thinking from unpleasant subjects to happy ones, it does something of equal importance. Normally, the man who pays the premiums on his life insurance puts his hand in his pocket with no prospect of a personal reward. But, put to him this way, he sees a reward and an immediate one.

Let me know what success you have with this idea, Mac.

Cordially,

IDEA FOR SALESMEN SELLING HIGH-PRICED MERCHANDISE

Build on weaknesses. If you know of common problems your salesmen face, give them the ability to convert weakness to strength.

Dear Tony,

You've been concerned about our prices, and I'd like to share some thoughts with you.

Sure, we charge more than most of our competitors. No question about it, if our prices were lower we would sell more machines. BUT . . . if our prices were lower, the difference would have to come out of the machines, our service or our pockets . . . the company's pockets, my pockets and your pockets. And, as you know, our percentage of profit is no greater than our lowest priced competitor's. The difference . . . and you know it . . . is in the quality of the equipment and the service behind it.

My guess is that you've been demonstrating our equipment, telling about its many fine features, extolling our service and, finally quoting price.

Ending your presentation with the price quotation, highlights it. When you rise from the dinner table, the flavor of the dessert lingers on. It is the last thing you tasted. Your prospects, impressed though they may be with our machines, are confronted, at the end of the presentation, with one thing . . . price. If they've done any shopping, they are thrown a bit because of the comparison, and everything else is buried under that final statement of price.

My suggestion is that you take the negative . . . price . . . and convert it to a positive.

Start with price. "Mr. Prospect, the machine I'm about to demonstrate to you costs $3400 . . . that's close to $400 more than most of our competitors, but when I have shown you its unusual features, its ruggedness and told you about our service organization, I think you'll agree that it's the most economical buy on the market."

Tony, I've done just that so many times I couldn't count them. It works. There's no shock at the close of the presentation. If there's a price objection at all, it is a weak, minor objection because you've been answering it throughout the demonstration.

Everyone knows that you get what you pay for. Your job is to show people that they get more when they buy our product. Price helps to prove your point.

When I see more sales on your record this month, I'll know why.

Cordially,

IDEA FOR SALESMEN WITH MULTIPLE LINES

Here is another idea intended to overcome a common weakness. And, once again, you wind-up your letter letting your salesmen know that you expect them to put the idea to work and to report on results.

Dear Charlie,

Do you agree with this? . . . the toughest part of your selling effort is that you have too much to offer.

Nobody knows better than I how true that is.

You go into a prospect's office with over a thousand items of office supplies to sell and where do you start?

Now, here's an idea . . .

Let the prospect *tell* you where to start. Don't laugh. That isn't as wild as it sounds. You can get him to do that for you easily.

Here's all you do. You get in to see Mr. Buyer and say, "Mr. Buyer, you have a complex job. The efficiency of many parts of this office depends, to a great extent, on you. I'm here with the hope that I can help you. Please look at this list and tell me where help is needed the most."

Here's the list you put in front of him:

I'm interested in greater economy and efficiency in . . .

filing
correspondence
shipping
storage
inter-company communications
clerical routine
inventory
production controls

You can add to that list if you see any holes, but don't make it too long. Type it on a 3 x 5 card and you've given yourself a potent sales weapon.

No matter what item he chooses, you have the opening you want and can pin-point your sales talk.

Put it to work, Charlie, and let's talk about the results next Monday morning.

Cordially,

IDEA TIED TO A NEW SALES AID

From time to time you equip your salesmen with new material to help them in their selling efforts. Sales aids are costly. They represent a great deal of thought, time, effort and cash. In many cases they are introduced with appropriate drama and enthusiasm, but they deserve continuing promotion to your salesmen . . . follow-through.

As is true with all phases of selling, observation and conversation will bring you a series of fresh thoughts on how to do something better, and this certainly applies to the use of sales aids.

The letter below promotes an idea that can be applied to many sales aids. If you think this or any other idea you transmit is particularly important, try the close this letter embraces. Telling a man that he's going to be called on to stand before his fellow salesmen to report on the effectiveness of an idea, literally forces him to use that idea as ably as he can.

Dear Jack,

The new sales aid you've been given does a beautiful job of telling our story. It dramatizes every key sales point in words and pictures. It leads right up to a close.

I've been asking some of the boys what happens when they come to the final page. Invariably they have told me what they start talking about at that point.

What do you talk about, Jack?

The book has told our story. Anything you say when the story has been told is bound to be repetitive. Don't you agree with me that, at the end of the presentation, our greatest interest should be . . . what *is the customer thinking?*

Unless we *know* what he's thinking any talking we do can be a costly distraction. It could lead him *away* from a sale.

How do we find out what he's thinking?

The answer is . . . with silence.

The next time you use the new presentation, when you reach the final page just sit with your lips sealed tight. Look at your prospect pleasantly and expectantly . . . BUT SAY NOTHING.

Difficult? No question about it. But it is even more difficult for your prospect. You've portrayed your story and now you are sitting there waiting for him to speak. The pressure is on him and he'll feel it.

What he says will tell you how to close the sale. He might even amaze you by saying he wants to buy.

Help me to prove the point, Jack. Use it between now and the next sales meeting. I'm going to call on you to tell how it works. I'm confident that it will work handsomely.

Thanks,

Ideas for a Salesman's Follow-Through

When you advance an idea, the essence of which can be told in a few words, it frequently pays to spotlight those few words in the physical form of your letter. Notice the indented paragraph in the next letter. The man, having read the entire letter, doesn't have to search for the key words ... the words he'll want to memorize.

Dear Al,

Everyone agrees that the open meetings for the public are proving to be the most effective means of creating sales we've ever tried. In an hour and a half we've been putting our message across to audiences that have averaged close to 100 people. Compare that with individual presentations and the time-saving factor is astronomical.

But, Al, the key to complete success is follow-through. We all know that.

Here's an idea.

Next Tuesday evening we have another show. You'll have close to 25 prospects there ... maybe a few more if the people you invited bring friends or relatives. During the coffee hour at the end of the meeting, you'll undoubtedly pick up a few firm appointments and you might even make some sales right then and there, as Andy and Mark did last week.

The vital point, however, is to follow-through with the others. The time to do it is Wednesday ... the day following the meeting, while the ideas are still fresh in their minds ... while the motivation to act is still strong.

So ... get on the phone Wednesday morning and stay with it until you've reached every prospect. And here's all you say ...

"I was so happy to see you at the meeting last night. Thanks for coming. Of all the ideas that were expressed, what interested you the most?"

Taking it from there is no problem. If your people tell you what interested them the most, you know exactly what to say and do to close sales.

Short ... sweet ... profitable.

Cordially,

In Summary . . . .

When writing letters to your salesmen to give them new selling ideas, you'll be more effective if you . . .

1. Convey the idea via personal, individually typed letters.
2. Compose your letters with the intent of selling your thoughts.
3. Start each letter with a statement addressed to the salesman's interests.
4. Make your thoughts clear and precise.
5. Bring your ideas to life by presenting believable situations.
6. Motivate salesmen to use your ideas by asking for result reports.
7. Show salesmen how to convert weaknesses to strengths.
8. Capitalize on your investments in sales aids by writing letters that offer new ideas on using them effectively.
9. Highlight key words or key thoughts in your letters by indenting, underscoring or the use of a second color.

16

Letters to Salesmen Who Are in a Slump or Unhappy

Salesmen in a slump

One of your most trying tasks is to rejuvenate a good salesman who has fallen by the wayside. The effort calls on your understanding of human nature and, in particular, on your understanding of the man involved.

Salesmen are individuals. There is no common cause that may be pinpointed when a man's sales and enthusiasm reach a low ebb. And if there is no common cause, there can be no common cure. Each case must be analyzed against the background of your knowledge of the man, his plusses and minuses, his background, home life, past record, ambitions, habits and more.

Sympathy and human understanding are required, of course, but they must be kept within bounds. When a salesman finds things going wrong he indulges in self pity. Too much sympathy from you can add to the handicap of self pity. What is needed, in most cases, is a small measure of sympathy mixed with a heaping measure of firmness.

Too Easily Satisfied

One common reason for a salesman falling into a slump is too much success combined with too little foresight and ambition. But just saying so won't change the man or the situation. The damage he is doing to himself must be made shockingly clear. Your showing of sympathy and under-standing should be revealed in the manner you adopt to point out the fault. The tone should be closer to that of a stern but loving father, rather than that of the outraged employer.

Dear George,

Picture yourself in charge of sending a rocket to the moon. After months of preparation it is ready to launch. At the end of the countdown it lifts off the pad, straight and true . . . beautiful . . . right on course . . . roaring off into space. Then, suddenly, half-way there, it loses power, falters . . . drops back to earth.

Can you imagine what your feelings would be?

I've had that feeling. You were the rocket, George. Now that the mission has petered out, after such a promising start, I've been reading the data to try to pin-point the cause of the wash-out and I think I've found it.

For the first six months you did a classical selling job. You covered your clients just as they should be covered. You brought in a great number of fine new accounts. You earned excellent commissions . . . the highest in your own history.

My conclusion is that you quit because you were satisfied. You'd earned enough to take care of your living needs for the year. You quit with the idea that when you need more money, all you have to do is turn on the steam again and it will be there waiting for you.

I don't think it will be waiting for you.

Business doesn't function that way, George. It doesn't for two reasons. Customers who have been neglected, don't remain customers very long. Salesmen who lose momentum . . . who have gotten accustomed to taking it easy . . . learn that it is immensely difficult to shed the easy life and start working again. The combination of the two leads to disappointments. Disappointments lead to negative attitudes. Negative attitudes lead to failure.

You have great gifts, George. That's been proven. You face a choice. You can use those gifts . . . rise to higher stations in life . . . do more for your family and yourself . . . build a reserve that can mean early re-tirement and financial security . . . or . . . you can turn your back on those gifts and let them waste away, passing up the fine rewards they promise.

All of us enjoy relaxation and recreation, but they must be earned. You haven't earned the amount of relaxation and recreation you are taking, George . . . you've only made a down payment.

Let's talk it over. I'm putting you on my calendar for noon lunch next Tuesday.

My best . . .

Rekindling a man's dreams can work wonders. Dreams, no matter how big and luring, can be submerged and lost from view by the daily pressures of life. But they are only submerged and are only temporarily out of sight. You, as sales manager, can bring those dreams back to the surface where they can again be seen . . . where they again can inspire and motivate.

The letter to Ralph does three important things; it brings the dream back to the surface . . . it appeals to his ego . . . it presents a challenge. When a man has expressed an ambition to another, and is reminded that he is being observed . . . is being measured . . . it is a difficult challenge to ignore.

Dear Ralph,

Three years and forty-two days ago we met for the first time. That's not memory. I keep records.

A few notes made on my memo about that meeting bring back many things. You weren't happy with the M Company because they put a ceiling on your earnings and opportunities. It was a ceiling you couldn't accept. You had ideas . . . dreams.

At the time you had a son . . . Ned. You and Mary wanted at least two more children. Now you have Ned and Ruth. You wanted to move from an apartment to a home. You pictured a rambler in the suburbs that you and Mary were going to build in keeping with your own ideas. And the next step was a vacation house up on the lake, with your own dock and a boat of your own.

You've done well, Ralph, as I thought you would. You're a fine salesman.

You have moved from the apartment and rented a two-story house in the suburbs. You have a late model car. Your family dresses well and eats well. And something else. You've become satisfied with what you have. You've become adjusted to doing a certain amount of work . . . enough work to support what you have today.

Does that rambler built to your own ideas . . . and Mary's ideas . . . look less attractive? Have you abandoned the lake home and the boat?

Ralph, the rambler, the place at the lake, the boat are well within your grasp. So many things that make life bright, exciting and wonderful are waiting for you. Not for everyone, by any means. They are there for you, though. I know it and you know it.

Sometimes clouds drift across dreams. But clouds move on. If there's any way I can help you to dispel those clouds, please give me your confidence for I'd honor it and give you all the help I can.

One of these days I want to be a guest in that vacation home and I want to skim across the lake with you in that boat of yours. And I don't want to wait too long.

My best . . .

ADVERSE PUBLICITY

There are times when an industry, or worse, an individual company, becomes the target of newspaper attacks. Whether the attacks are justified or not, the depressing effect on a sales organization can be devastating. It is a time for quick action. The reaction of the sales force must be channeled in positive directions before negative thoughts take root.

Dear Sam,

There's no question about it . . . we've taken some terrible abuse from the press.

The hearings that took place in Washington became a field day for the newspapers. They made headlines out of the sharpest questions and few of them bothered to report out industry's excellent responses.

When those stories first appeared, I was sick. But not any more.

The reason I recovered . . . completely and quickly. . . . is that I decided to research a hunch, and I have found out that I was right.

My hunch was that only two groups of people read those stories with any interest and attention . . . those of us in the business and our customers. Our customers know what they have. They are happy with the results they've enjoyed and questions in Washington aren't going to change their satisfaction. Biased headlines aren't going to change their knowledge of their personal experiences one bit. But what about the people we haven't sold . . . the people we will be approaching in the days ahead?

These people had little or no interest in the subject . . . they aren't involved. Few men read every story in every edition of the papers. They scan headlines and read the stories concerned with those things that are meaningful to them.

Even those who have read the articles will have forgotten them within a few days. Not being involved, they have no reason to remember.

I had our advertising agency do a quick "man in the street" survey and *my hunch was right.*

Sam, if you read those stories and said to yourself, "This is terrible. With this kind of publicity nobody will buy" . . . you are absolutely right. If you read them and said, "These stories are rough, but if I run into any prospects who raise the same questions I can easily provide the answers and document them, therefore this shouldn't hurt sales one bit" . . . you are absolutely right.

All I'm saying is that your mental attitude is the only thing that counts. If you go out with your usual enthusiasm and confidence, business will be as good as ever. If you take a hang-dog attitude and expect to be licked, you will be licked.

Rise above the bad press we've had, Sam. It is over. It is behind us. Let's not prolong any effect it may have had by clinging to it. Go out and SELL.

My best . . .

BAD ECONOMIC CONDITIONS

It is normal and natural for sales to follow broad economic trends. But decreasing sales have a bad habit of snowballing. Once a salesman becomes convinced that business is going to be bad, he is inclined to lower his efforts, feeling that whatever he does will prove fruitless . . . *unless* you, as his sales manager, convince him that a falling economy can represent opportunity for the man who makes an extra effort.

Dear Cliff,

We all read the reports. The economy is in a down trend right now. Inventories are up, buying is down, the public isn't spending, unemployment is rising and it will be a while before the pendulum starts swinging in the other direction.

Okay . . . let's start selling.

I've been working at sales and with salesmen long enough to know what happens during such periods. There are two types of salesmen. One group says, "Business is lousy, so why try?" and the other group says, "Business is lousy so I'll have to try harder."

And here's the joker . . .

There are so many in the first group that those in the second group often do better than they ever did before. The competition has left them a wide-open field.

Almost anyone can look like a good salesman when business is booming. The real test of a man is how well he can perform when conditions aren't good. A good man sharpens his skills on adversity and when the good days come back he becomes a real star.

These are more than mere words, Cliff.

In my estimation you have the qualities to become a star. You've demonstrated that in many ways. This is your real opportunity. Make all you can of it and the time will come when you'll be thankful that this slump came along.

Cordially,

A SERIES OF BAD BREAKS AND DISAPPOINTMENTS

The best of salesmen will run into periods peppered with failure. And selling is lonely work. At each crucial sales interview the man is unsupported . . . alone. He becomes acutely aware of his lonely status during hard luck periods. But when he knows that his sales manager is keenly aware of his trying circumstances . . . that your faith in him remains at a high level . . . it becomes much easier for him to break out of the losing streak.

A negative attitude is easy to detect. When you recognize it, act quickly to give the suffering salesman the reassurance he wants and needs.

Dear Chuck,

I know what you are going through. It's rough.

For months you've had a series of disappointments and bad breaks. There seems no end to it and it is mighty depressing.

The worst thing about a prolonged sales slump is that it feeds on itself. Day after day of unhappy results inevitably develops an attitude of defeat. You go out each day anticipating poor business. And no matter how well you may think you hide that attitude from the people you visit . . . it can't be done. Somehow, in some way, it comes through. People feel it and react. They mirror your own negativism.

Changing a mental attitude is not easy, but it can and must be done.

There are few powers within us more powerful than the power of believing. Just one illustration . . .

Ever since track records were kept no man ever ran the mile in less than four minutes. This was a well established fact that was known and believed by all who competed for that event. Then, in 1954 a man by the name of Roger Bannister broke the record. He ran the mile in less than four minutes. Once it was proven that it could be done . . . once track stars believed it possible . . . many men have run the mile in less than four minutes.

Chuck, tomorrow has no relationship to today, yesterday or all the days gone by. Tomorrow is a brand-new day full of brand-new opportunities for you. You know you can sell and can sell well. Tomorrow is the day when you can regain your momentum, your enthusiasm, your belief in yourself.

Believe it, Chuck. It is true. We both know it. Believe it.

Cordially,

Too Much Time Spent with Friendly Customers

One evidence of the aforementioned loneliness in a salesman's life often rises to the surface when you see him devoting more and more time to well established accounts. This occurs, most often, when sales are off. Simply telling a man to change such habits won't be nearly as effective as leading him to an understanding of the spurious rationalizations and the waste involved.

Dear Hal,

A certified public accountant can take a financial statement and read in it things that the rest of us can't see. He can quickly pin-point trouble spots and suggest solutions.

Happily, I've been reading sales reports long enough to have developed a similar knack. You've been having some problems lately, and I've just been reading your reports. They show me where the trouble is.

Mart Johnson and George Palmer are two of your best customers. They've both been giving you excellent business for many years. You've developed a fine relationship with them and bend over backwards to give them good service. Good. That's as it should be.

Last year, from January through June, business was good. You were bringing in many new accounts and you won the monthly sales contest twice during that period. In the latter part of the year your sales began to slack off and have continued to go downhill during the first half of this year.

Your January to June sales reports for last year show that 18% of your sales calls were to Mart Johnson and George Palmer. But this year 42% of your calls were made to those two customers. Neither is buying any more than they do normally.

Here's why. When the going got rough, you went through a period where you had a lot of rejections. Your friends Mart and George were what I call "comfort havens." No rejections there. You know you can visit them and you'll be well received. You can justify those increased calls to yourself. You are giving good customers extra service and attention.

Now let's face the truth, Hal.

Those men don't require that much attention and there's even a good chance that they may secretly wish you didn't take up so much of their business time. They like and admire you so they won't say so. And . . . this is the vital point . . . every extra call you make on them robs you of the opportunity to see new prospects and to make new friends . . . new customers.

No more "comfort havens," Hal. I'm not asking that you write to tell me I'm right. But confess it to yourself and shift gears.

Cordially,

Salesmen's complaints

Most good salesmen are also good gripers. The ambition and the nervous energy that carry them to heights in selling also goad them to want changes. Their creativeness leads them to ideas that may be expressed to you as complaints.

A salesman's complaints are as important as those emanating from customers. Both must be answered with thoughtful consideration. To brush off a salesman's complaint with a brief refusal creates a wound that may not heal. If his complaint, in your considered judgment, must be refused, your reply should reflect your understanding. The reasons for your refusal must be given in sufficient detail for him to appreciate the thought you have given to the question. He may not be happy, but he won't be resentful.

THE REQUEST FOR MORE TERRITORY

The next field always does look greener, and requests for new or extra territory are common. But the desire for room to work does reveal ambition and energy and, even if it is to be refused, a recognition of those qualities goes a long way in placating the man who made the request.

Dear Gary,

It was with a good measure of understanding and sympathy that I read your letter this morning. Your desire for more territory is a credit to you. It pleases me that you have the desire to grow.

Your letter took me back, Gary. Not so very many years ago I covered New York City for another firm in our field. One day I came into my sales manager and asked if I might have New Jersey and Connecticut. I'd been working New York for a long time and was convinced that I could build my sales substantially if I had Jersey and Connecticut.

He didn't say yes or no, but that he'd think it over and let me know.

Two weeks later he called me in. On his desk was a list of better than 1400 possible outlets for our line in New York City. Another list showed that New Jersey and Connecticut together had about 700 possible outlets and a final list was a summary of my own call reports in New York. I had visited a little better than 400 prospects in New York.

He didn't say a word. He just pushed the lists at me and sat back.

After studying the lists for a few minutes, I looked up at him. We both smiled and I walked out. My sales hit a new high that same year because I added so many new accounts.

Gary, your request proves to me that you are human and that you are ambitious. The human quality makes the next field look greener. The ambition will spur you to make more of what you have after you review the lists I've enclosed.

My best . . .

The Request for Lower Prices

A man faced with difficult price competition each working day easily can lose perspective. If he hears a number of people singing the same song, he'll begin to hum the tune. The handling of such a complaint calls for a firm reply. But notice how this letter, despite a total lack of agreement with the request, starts out in step with the salesman by saying, "You are right."

Dear Quint,

You are right. If we became competitive with the J.B. Company by matching their prices, we'd increase sales. To do so, however, we'd have to change some other thing or things. The difference would have to come out of our product, our services, your commission rate or company profits. The percentage of profit the company makes is in line with the J.B. Company and most of our leading competitors.

For years you have been doing a great job with our line despite the lower prices of J.B. and a half dozen other firms. How? You and I know how. You've successfully shown that we have more to offer and that the extra measures of quality and service are well worth the difference.

Quint, they're still worth the difference, and then some.

The fact that we are leaders in our field even though our prices are higher is a powerful selling point. You've let somebody sell you that the opposite is true. Resell yourself, Quint. You know the facts.

Your biggest customers and your best prospects don't buy price. They buy what our goods and support will do for them. The buyer who looks at price alone is never a desirable customer. He's fair game for anyone who will sell for a little less next time, regardless of all other considerations. He doesn't survive very long.

Take pride in what our prices represent. You offer the best.

Cordially,

The Request for Leads from Advertising

When a salesman evidences a desire for help in an area where he should be capable of helping himself, he clearly is in need of strong guidance. Bert, in the next letter, is given a complete explanation as to why his request will not be fulfilled. More importantly, however, his sales manager, quite properly, accepts the blame for the lack of understanding and spells out what steps will be taken to correct the omission.

Dear Bert,

Thanks for your letter, Bert. It means a lot to me when you unburden yourself to me for it is much healthier than your harboring any dissatisfaction. If we always are frank with one another, we'll grow together instead of growing apart.

You've said that you are unhappy because we don't do more national space and direct mail advertising so that we can supply you with a greater flow of leads.

Bert, the most vital possession you have is your time . . . the time spent face-to-face with people who are well qualified prospects and who have the ability to buy. The prime question is, how do you find such people?

Experience over many years has given us the answer.

Advertising does, indeed, produce leads. But we've learned that such leads generally prove to be of poor quality. Many are idly curious . . . , a good percentage are children . . . a surprising number come from interested competitors and a good number are from people who are sincerely interested but don't have the means to take action . . . the dreamers.

On the other hand, experience also has demonstrated that the leads our salesmen generate from asking customers for referrals are, in most cases, extremely well qualified.

There isn't a single man in the upper ten percent of our sales force who ever worries about leads. Every one of our top producers lives on referrals. If we gave him leads from advertising, the chances are he'd ignore them because he doesn't have the time to call on suspects when he has so many prospects.

You've been taught how to ask for and to get good referrals. Your request for company produced leads tells me that you aren't using the lessons you were taught. And maybe that's my fault. Maybe we didn't teach it properly and failed to convince you that this is the soundest route to follow.

Next week Harry will be in your territory and I'm asking him to spend a few days working with you, concentrating on the development of your referral-getting technique. He's a master at it and he can make you a master at it, too.

Cordially,

The Threat to Leave for Bigger Commissions

Selling a salesman on staying with you when he has virtually decided to accept the lure of bigger commissions elsewhere, is no simple task. But it can be done. As demonstrated in the letter to Mitch, it requires a complete review of the many elements working in favor of the salesman for your firm as opposed to a consideration of commission rates alone.

Dear Mitch,

As I'm sure you anticipated, your letter has caused considerable concern.

You've been doing an outstanding job. We've been delighted with you and the progress you've made and I had assumed that the feeling was mutual. Obviously, I've been wrong, for now you are talking about leaving us because you can get higher commissions from a competitor.

Our commission schedule was not arrived at idly. It resulted from years of experience, study, trial and error. It is a formula that was developed for us by a management consultant group who were armed with complete information about competing rates and factors. They and our own executive committee are satisfied that the earning opportunities available to our sales force are generous and fully competitive.

Until this time the bulk of the men we have lost to the lure of slightly higher commission scales were those who weren't making the grade and thought that fatter commissions would solve their problems. They never do.

A man selling an unknown or unreliable product with a 50% commission won't make as much as a man who sells a highly regarded, nationally respected product at 10% commission.

I don't know what firm you have been talking with and it doesn't matter. I do know . . . and so do you . . . that your representation of us is a huge asset to you. Our reputation for quality, integrity, for dealer cooperation and fair pricing are money in your own bank account. They make your work easier. They open doors for you. They enable you to do your work with pride and confidence.

You know the high calibre of our sales force. You must know, too, how every one of them has been wined, dined and wooed by other firms in and out of our field. Rarely have we lost one of our successful men in that way, and a few who did succumb have come back.

Mitch, we're sold on the soundness of our commission schedule and we never have and never will alter it for any individual. I urge you to weigh all of the factors and not look at just one element . . . commissions . . . isolated from the important rest. If you will, I think you'll feel, as I do, that your fine performance and your excellent commission income to date is no more than an indication of how far you can go in your present position. No ceilings have been put above you and they never will be.

I hope I'll have your reply that you've thought it through and have decided that your future is with us.

Cordially,

In Summary . . . .

When writing to salesmen in a slump or responding to their complaints, your letters will accomplish more if you . . .

1. Think of and treat each man as an individual.
2. Be sympathetic, but keep it within bounds.
3. Be the stern but loving father—not the outraged employer.
4. Rekindle men's own dreams.
5. Be quick to overcome adverse publicity.
6. Show salesmen that bad economic conditions can spell opportunity.
7. Show your unfailing faith in a man who's been having a series of disappointments.
8. Be on the alert for a man devoting increasing time to friendly customers.
9. Answer a salesman's complaint with the care you'd give to a complaint from a customer.
10. In refusing a request from a salesman, demonstrate the thought given to the request and expand on the reasons for refusal.

17

Letters That Discipline Salesmen

In the previous chapter, the observation was made that a salesman has the loneliest job in the world. Loneliness, if it becomes extreme, will reduce a man's spirit and, in consequence, his ability to sell. This, in itself, is a potent reason for you to impose discipline on your sales force. When you lay down rules, telling a man what he must do . . . when he must do it . . . how often he must do it, he knows that he is not alone. You and your admonishments are present. You are guiding him and shaping his career. He doesn't feel neglected.

A number of years ago the Sales and Marketing Executives sponsored a survey of salesmen and one of the key questions asked of thousands of active, successful salesmen, was to check their first, second and third choices on a list of things they wanted more of to make them happier in their work. The list included such items as higher commissions, more territory, longer vacations, greater recognition, etc. To everyone's astonishment the biggest vote was . . . more *supervision.*

Supervision is just another word for discipline. Salesmen want the comforting knowledge that you have them in mind, are watching their actions and that you care.

Letters demanding discipline, therefore, can play a key role in your efforts to make your sales force stronger, more effective, happier and more enduring.

Discipline can be thrust upon salesmen by your issuing tough, brief communications stating that they will do this, that or the other thing . . . or else. But handling the problem in that manner can do more harm than good. It creates no image of thoughtful cooperation and a sincere desire to help a man in his career.

You are dealing with intelligent people and intelligent people respond best to discipline and supervision that details the reasons why certain rules are made and enforced.

Poor Paper Work

In the following letter, salesman Frans is told that he must stop handling his report writing in a careless, indifferent manner, but it is presented to him in a manner calculated to make him want to follow orders. While the letter is firm, it clearly demonstrates a genuine interest in Frans' welfare.

Dear Frans,

Salesmen are individualists, but there's one thing they have in common . . . they all hate paper work.

And there's one other fact that has proven to be true . . . the most successful salesmen are those who are willing to do the things they dislike.

You have been consistent in demonstrating your personal dislike of paper work. Your reports to me have been irregular and those that do come in are incomplete.

Frans, I share your dislike of paper work, but I respect it. I know how important it is. Because I always have and still do find paper work a bore and a bother, I have made every effort to ask for an absolute minimum from you and the others on the sales team.

The reports I require are more important to you than they are to me. Any salesman who works without written plans and written records is rudderless. He can't see where he's going and he can't examine the log to see where he has been. Orderly records can tell you invaluable stories. They can show areas of strength and areas of weakness. They can help you to eliminate or reduce unprofitable time usage and they can help you to make your success a greater one.

You are a good salesman, Frans. With your cooperation I can help you become a great salesman. In the past I have asked, cajoled and kidded you about making your weekly plans and your weekly results sheets a must. Now I'm going to insist. To do less . . . to continue to permit you to let this vital work slide . . . would be doing *you* an injustice.

From now on, plan to put aside just a single hour on Saturday or Sunday to thoughtfully write your plan for the week ahead and to complete your call report sheet for the week past. Put your copies in your binders and mail my copies so that they'll be on my desk Monday or Tuesday.

But, Frans, don't stop there. You're going to be doing this to help yourself grow. Review your own reports searchingly. Dig out the evidences of good practices and of bad ones. Let the reports of the past mould the plans for the weeks ahead. The facts are there to be seen and interpreted. I'll be sending you my comments, too. Stick with this discipline, Frans, and I promise you that a year from now you'll be well ahead financially and will be enjoying your work even more.

You'll even learn to enjoy the little bit of paper work involved.

My best . . .

LAZINESS

Discipline can be sold. The habit of being lazy is a difficult one to overcome. But knowing your man . . . knowing what he wants out of life . . . is the *need* you can concentrate on. Once you've established a need and show how it can be served by adopting new habits, you have a good chance of making the sale.

Dear Maury,

Last week the newspapers were full of feature stories about one of the big labor unions winning a 5% increase for their members. It was big news.

Now I have some news for you.

How would you like a 15% increase in your earnings? It is yours if you want it. I'm completely serious. You've been earning a fairly good commission income. You sell well . . . but you don't sell hard. You have adopted a leisurely pace for yourself and it is evident in your call reports.

It is as simple as this, Maury . . . increase the time you spend face-to-face with customers and potential customers and, inevitably, you'll earn 15% more income.

I've been looking at your records for the past several months, and contrasting them with just about every successful man on the sales force. You average 15% fewer calls. You start late and you end each day early.

I suspect that you've built a mental trap for yourself.

We all enjoy some extra leisure and the luxury of getting up late and coming home early. And it is so easy to kid yourself into believing that this isn't being lazy, but that buyers don't like to see salesmen at the start or the close of the day. But it just isn't true. Many of the people we sell to are in their offices at seven-thirty or eight in the morning. No phones are ringing. Their own employees are rarely there. It is a relaxed period when a man can give fuller attention to a good presentation. By four in the afternoon most of the "must" jobs for the day are out of the way. The pressure of the day is off. Not as many salesmen are knocking at the door. Another relaxed period.

I know how ambitious you are to live a good life . . . to give your family every luxury. Start moving up the economic ladder, Maury . . . now. Help yourself to that 15% boost in your standard of living. It's there waiting for you. Habits are easy to form and easy to change.

Start tomorrow morning. I'll be watching your reports for those extra calls and I'm confident that I'll see them.

My best . . .

Taking Orders Instead of Selling

The man whose records reveal a lack of activity in putting effective sales aids to work, needs discipline. He's either taking the easy path in his work or he is pitting his judgment against your own. The letter to Chester spells out the weakness and demands action in a manner that puts him on notice that his response will be measured.

Dear Chester,

Knowing how conscientious you are, I'm sure that you are as concerned as I am about the trend your sales have taken. You've been working hard . . . seeing lots of people . . . but your orders have been unusually small.

There's really no mystery to this and you can change that trend with ease.

Reviewing your records reveals a pattern. I've seen it before and I've seen it corrected before. It is simply this . . . your customers have been doing the selling . . . not you.

Two factors spell it out. Nationally, sales are up. That's number one. The second factor is that you are making sales to as many people as ever, only the amount of each sale is below normal.

Let's face the facts, Chester, you've been taking orders instead of merchandising. We have a broad line to offer. We have developed proven plans that help merchants to move our goods. We are backing them up with window and point-of-purchase displays and racks that feature our lines effectively.

It has been a long time since you have ordered out any of the great sales aids available to you. The answer is clear, isn't it? You've been by-passing these resultful routes to bigger sales. You've been taking the easier path . . . simply asking what they want . . . taking orders.

Now, let's change all of that. Starting now, make your calls with the determination that your chief role is to help your customers to sell more of our goods . . . to make more profits for themselves. You are the expert with the tools and the knowledge that can bring them extra business. Stop taking orders and start making sales.

From today on I'll be on the watch for your requests for sales aids to be shipped to specific customers. I want to see several of them each week and I want to see in your reports, the actions you are taking to make those sales supports work.

Cordially,

Antagonistic to Customers

When a man's letters and reports indicate a growing attitude of resentment concerning his customers, it is a danger signal that should not be ignored. Not infrequently the man, himself, may be unaware of this development and the sooner it is exposed for his own analysis the more you can help him to correct the situation. The final paragraph in the letter to Tom carries a practical suggestion and the suggestion in itself helps to emphasize your concern.

Dear Tom,

The letter you wrote last Saturday just reached me. Some of your comments struck a familiar chord and I went to the files and pulled out a half dozen of your more recent letters. As I thought, they have a consistent theme. It is a theme that concerns me deeply and a theme that explains the slump you've been in.

Every time you have written in recent months, you have made disparaging remarks about customers. So-and-so is a crank . . . this one is stupid . . . another is a chronic fault finder and still another expects too much service.

Maybe your customers are not all nature's noblemen. Few of us are. We all have our faults. But, Tom, I find it hard to believe that nearly everyone you call on is mean, unpleasant or unintelligent. They have their good points and their bad ones. They have good moods and bad moods. They are human.

Tom, you make a good living. You have a lovely home, a new car; you and your family eat well and dress well. All of this because of those customers. They make possible all of your worldly goods. You have a lot to thank them for.

Be understanding and sympathetic to the customer in a sour mood. His mood is what it is because something unhappy has happened at his office or his home. If a customer is slow to understand, be grateful that the good Lord blessed you with intelligence. Share it with him. Help him. If another is over-demanding of service, be happy that it is you he looks to for help . . . not a competitor.

If we look for faults, we'll find them. If we look for traits to admire and to like, we'll find them with equal ease. And . . . above all . . . never forget that whatever we feel . . . antagonism or affection . . . will be evident to those we deal with no matter how much we try to hide our feelings.

Sometimes, Tom, a bitter attitude stems from little more than bad digestion or some equally simple physical ailment. Please do yourself the important favor of seeing your doctor for a check-up. You are not a bitter person. Your attitude toward the people you have every reason to like is a symptom that something is out of kilter. Let's get to the source and lick it.

Please let me know.

Cordially,

Non-Attendance at Sales Meetings

Skipping planned sales meetings is a symptom of something seriously wrong. Even if a salesman considers the meetings a bore and a waste of time, it should not be his prerogative to decide whether he should or should not attend. You plan those meetings for a practical purpose and the men who stay away not only weaken themselves, but set a bad example for others.

Dear Andy,

You've missed three out of the last five sales meetings and I wonder why.

Our meetings are planned to provide you with facts and ideas that will help you to grow. If you deliberately deprive yourself of this means of fortifying your selling efforts, you are handicapping yourself. Nor is getting the gist of what was covered from one of your fellow salesmen any substitute for being there where you would be given the details in depth . . . where you could ask questions, raise objections or give the rest of us the benefit of your own observations and experience.

You are important to those meetings, and they are important to you.

The finest salesmen living require new thoughts, fresh inspiration and current product knowledge if they are to continue to be fine salesmen.

Skipping the meetings can become a habit. Attending meetings can become a habit. One hurts and the other helps.

Andy, if something comes up that makes it impossible or seriously inconvenient to be at a scheduled meeting, get in touch with me in advance. Otherwise, I'll count on your attending the meetings from now on.

Cordially,

Discourtesy to Customer

When a customer takes the time and trouble to tell you of an instance of discourtesy on the part of one of your salesmen, you have some severe problems. One of the biggest problems is your own self-control. If the salesman is worth retaining, you'll be working against your own best interests if you follow your instincts and vent your well justified anger at him. This could be particularly dangerous if you have not had the chance to hear the salesman's side of the story.

Your man has been guilty . . . or seems to have been guilty . . . of a serious offense. Your job is to make him realize his error and the need to humble himself by apologizing at once. You also want the episode to be the last of its kind, so your letter must show him the folly of permitting himself to express himself in a discourteous manner no matter how great the provocation.

Dear Bert,

Just a few moments ago I had a phone call from Mr. Bolt of Jones & Co. He blistered me for about ten minutes about your actions in his office this afternoon.

I gather that he had made an appointment with you and kept you waiting for a half hour. When he saw you, he claims, you were extremely discourteous. You told him that your time was too valuable to spend in his waiting room, and, I gather, you said a good deal more.

Although I haven't heard your side of the story, I apologized profusely.

Your side of the story is of interest to me. I definitely want to hear it. But, Bert, there is never any excuse for discourtesy. If you sincerely feel that a customer has been inconsiderate and impolite, you have every right to retain your dignity and to take what measures you can to avoid any duplication of such treatment. You can do that, however, without ever being abusive and ungentlemanly. There is always a pleasant, intelligent way to convey an idea.

To respond to discourtesy with discourtesy is childish and foolish.

Every time you talk with a customer or a prospect, you represent the company as well as yourself. You may get momentary gratification telling a man off, but both you and the firm can pay dearly for that moment of satisfaction for years to come.

Unless there is much more to the story than I have heard, I'm asking you to reach Mr. Bolt in person, or on the phone immediately, and offer him a full and sincere apology. You'll be a bigger person for doing so, in your own esteem, in mine and in Mr. Bolt's.

Let me know what happens before the end of the week.

Cordially,

In Summary . . . .

Your letters that are intended to discipline salesmen will be more resultful if you . . .

1. Accept the fact that salesmen need and want discipline.
2. Salesmen are intelligent people and will respond better to orders that are fully explained as opposed to curt demands.
3. Letters of discipline should reflect a sincere desire to help the individual.
4. Sell the discipline you want to enforce.
5. Let the man know that his future actions will be checked.
6. Advise specific steps to help a man to overcome a problem.
7. Insist on immediate corrective action when a salesman has offended a customer.

18

Letters of Pep and Praise

Letters of Praise

CONSISTENT PRODUCTION

Dear Nick,

Every once in a while an order that's exceptionally big hits my desk . . . or one of the boys wins a wonderful new account . . . or something else sensational happens. And there are always cheers and wholehearted congratulations.

But, Nick, these once in a while exciting victories, as welcome as they are, don't mean as much as month-after-month consistent production.

I just wanted you to know how fully and deeply I appreciate your splendid work. I think you're great.

My best . . .

You'll see one vivid contrast when you move from the previous chapters to this one. Most of the letters of praise and pep are short. The one above is typical. When selling an idea . . . when trying to encourage a discouraged salesman and when writing about disciplinary matters, short letters, in most cases, would be wrong. There is too much ground to cover.

When you have reason to pat a man on the back, however, you can be breezy and brief.

But while letters of recognition for good work can be brief, the results will be long. Everyone wants to be appreciated. All of us thrive on sincere praise. And all of us are inclined to harbor a degree of resentment if we have reason to feel that hard work and conscientious efforts seem to be taken for granted or ignored.

The letter to Nick, enthusing about his consistent production, is likely to be particularly well received. It is an unexpected type of letter, not triggered by anything out of the ordinary. It would, therefore, be an unordinary man who, on receiving such a letter, would fail to glow with pleasure and feel that his sales manager is quite a wonderful guy.

LANDING A BIG ACCOUNT

While the winning of new customers is somewhat routine for a salesman, bringing in a big one is an occasion for celebration. A success of that type is doubly gratifying to the salesman . . . the extra income it represents and the confirmation of his selling skills. The victory is blunted, however, if the home office fails to show recognition of achievement.

Dear Herman,

You and Mary should have had quite a victory celebration last week. Congratulations on landing that great new account. I know how much thought, effort and talent you put into the work that won it for you.

I'm thrilled for you and I know that there will be more to follow. You're a real pro.

My best . . .

HOLDING A BIG ACCOUNT

Your appreciation of a man's ability to overcome a competitor's efforts to take away an important customer can mean as much to the salesman as the triumph itself. In the congratulatory letter to Lloyd, the stress is on the salesman's abilities, rather than on the importance to the company of keeping the income the customer represents.

Dear Lloyd,

You're a magician!

For weeks I've been watching your struggle to hold on to the Jones Company account and I knew what you were up against. Terrific odds were pitted against you. It looked like a lost cause several times.

But you did it.

Lloyd, you can take more pride in that accomplishment than if you had brought in ten new accounts. The next time we're together I want a blow-by-blow description because I'm sure I can learn a lot from the way you handled an immensely difficult situation.

My greatest respect and sincerest congratulations.

Cordially,

THE WELL-ORGANIZED MAN

Another unexpected type of letter is one that lauds a man for something other than actual sales. Soundly organized salesmen are relatively rare. When a man is flattered by being asked to address his fellow salesmen as an expert on a sales related subject it does three things . . . it gives him a great measure of satisfaction . . . it fortifies an existing strength . . . it helps the rest of the sales force when they listen to one of their fellows on such a subject, as opposed to hearing the same thing from you or another executive.

Dear Owen,

Please do me a great favor.

When we have our national sales meeting in August, I'd like you to conduct a twenty-minute discussion on time control.

There isn't a man in our sales organization as capable of thoughtful programming as you. I've been admiring your great skills in this area for a long time. You know the value of your time and you channel it with brilliance. It shows in your earnings, too.

If the whole group can pick up just a portion of your fine ideas, Owen, the sales meeting will pay great dividends for all of us.

Cordially,

Contest Winner

Contests have great values. After each contest, however, sales have an unhappy habit of sliding back to normal. Your congratulatory letter to a contest winner . . . and to the runners-up, as well . . . can help to overcome that dip. The final paragraph of the letter to Milt attempts to do just that.

Dear Milt,

Congratulations, winner!

You really romped home with the big prize. I fully appreciate the enormous amount of hard work, time and thought that went into the fabulous selling you did to come out on top. The competition was huge.

And, Milt, you won much more than the first prize.

You won the respect of every man and woman in our whole company. You, unquestionably, became an even bigger hero to your grand family. You stand even higher in the esteem of your customers.

But there's an even more important reward.

You now have, more than ever before, reason to know your own competence. How wonderful to be able to look to the future with such assurance of continuing growth and success. That is the biggest prize.

Cordially,

Contest Leader

In a prolonged contest it can be important to maintain momentum. Enthusiastic letters to those who are out in front lets them know that their successful efforts are appreciated and can inspire them to even greater effort.

Dear Randy,

Are you as excited as I am about the contest?

I've just been going over the record to date and had to tell you how beautiful a job I think you're doing.

A lot can happen during the remaining weeks and your dazzling performance probably will inspire some of the others to try even harder, but your results to date must be wonderfully gratifying to you.

Keep it up, Randy. The best of luck to you.

My best . . .

SALESMAN WITH IDEAS

The man in the field, seeing what happens with your products on the firing line, often is the first to see the need for change or improvement. Every idea he sends in may not be acceptable, but it can pay off handsomely if he is encouraged to keep his eyes, ears and mind open for product or merchandising improvements.

Dear Stu,

What a magnificent idea.

When your letter came to me, I hurried right down to production and we spent most of the day discussing it. It's in the hands of the engineers now and I'm staying right on top of it.

I'll keep you posted on the development.

Everyone is excited about the innovation, Stu, and I congratulate you on a great concept.

Cordially,

When You Are Appreciated

Once in a long while one of your salesmen will do the unusual and will pat *you* on the back for something. Make it a two-way street. Whenever one of your men is that considerate, hurry to let him know of *your* appreciation of his thoughtfulness.

Dear Ron,

You warm my heart.

Salesmen are wonderful people. They're always thinking, innovating, looking for better ways to do things. Part of the result is that the sales manager is on the receiving end of a relentless flow of demands, gripes and requests for change. It's to be expected.

Just once in a long while someone out in the field takes the time to say, "I like that."

It's a glorious feeling.

Thanks for being one of those rare people.

Gratefully,

Pep Letters

It is no easy task for the man in the field to maintain enthusiasm day after day. Moods and doubts and even boredom are enemies that must be fought constantly. Your recognition of this can inspire a flow of letters calculated to help your people to bolster their enthusiasm for their company and the goods they sell.

New Product Coming

While it is usually good strategy to keep a new product under wraps until you have your force together for a well planned presentation, the reception the presentation gets can be strengthened if you send word ahead that there is a new item in the making. It is your means of stoking the fires of enthusiasm so that they will burst forth into bright flames when the big day comes.

Dear Ned,

By now you've received the special notice about the meeting to be held Saturday morning, but I wanted to add this personal note.

At that meeting you are going to get the full details and you will see a new product that will make Sunday the longest day in your life. You won't be able to wait for Monday to come so that you can get out and tell the world what you have.

Wait till you see!

Cordially,

Expanded Territory

When a man is to be given additional territory, make a big event of it. Let your letter reveal your personal enthusiasm for the broader opportunities afforded. Give him knowledgeable guidance and support. Tell him of his own fine qualities that encouraged you to give him added responsibilities and greater chances to add to his personal income.

Dear Dave,

Great news, Dave.

From now on your territory will include Area S-11. It's a beautiful opportunity for you to make substantial additions to your sales and your income.

With this letter I'm giving you two lists . . . the customers we now serve and their annual volume figures for the past three years . . . and a list of the prime prospects waiting for you to convert them to customers.

You've kept yourself fully occupied covering your present territory. Now is the time to sit down and to do some creative reviewing. This is the opportunity to upgrade. My suggestion is that you divide your current customers into three categories . . . very profitable, fairly profitable and not profitable. Unless you have sound reason to anticipate that those in the unprofitable category can be moved upward, drop them. Plan how you'll handle those in the fairly profitable group in a manner that will make fewer demands on your time. I don't think you'll want to reduce your service to the top group and I'm sure it won't be necessary.

It all adds up to this . . . you'll be devoting more of your time to top profit accounts from now on.

Next week a letter will go out to all customers and prospects in your new territory. It will introduce you, paving the way for your initial calls. Thanks for being the kind of a man that will permit me to write a glowing letter. You'll get a copy as soon as it's composed.

The best of luck with the expansion, Dave. I'm delighted for you.

Cordially,

INTRODUCING A NEW SALES AID

Capitalize on the investment in a new sales aid. If the unit is good it will speak for itself, but if *you* speak for it your men are going to accept it with greater eagerness. When a new aid is being planned and created, many considerations are weighed. By the time it has been completed those considerations are well defined in your mind. Your salesmen, however, haven't had the exposure to the unit that you have enjoyed. Some benefits that may seem obvious to you may go unnoticed when the item reaches your people.

Plan your letter of announcement as carefully as you planned the unit. Spell out its virtues and your own concepts as to how it can be employed in the most profitable manner.

Dear Earle,

A big package was mailed to you this morning.

It is big in dimensions but immensely bigger in what it will mean to you in increased sales.

For months we've been working with the advertising agency in the development of a new point-of-purchase display stand. At last it has been completed. The package coming to you carries 6 of the new displays and will carry you to new heights of enthusiasm.

You've never seen a more handsome, attractive, self-selling unit. The dealers who use it will increase their own prestige as well as ours. My guess is that everyone you show it to will ask, "How soon can I have one?"

Here's a suggestion . . .

When the package arrives, set one up and study it thoroughly. Then take out your account list and determine how much extra merchandise you should recommend to each customer on the strength of this potent new sales maker.

Next, review your list of prime prospects and decide which ones will decide to become customers when they see this powerful new support that is head and shoulders over anything any of our competition offers.

Then GO!

My best . . .

Management Reports

Is a voluminous management report about to go out to the entire sales force? Undoubtedly, in it there is a great deal of meaty information that your salesmen should read and absorb. But heavy reports frequently get put aside or are read hurriedly and carelessly.

Pave the way for the report. If you are sold that the contents merit full and thoughtful reading, an advance letter alerting the sales force to what is coming and why they should read thoroughly, can make a substantial difference.

Dear Greg,

How I wish you could have been with me at the all-day session I attended yesterday. Jeff Hunter, our President, conducted a seven-hour seminar that brought together the heads of all departments of the company to discuss plans for the coming year.

I've sat in on sessions like this in the past, but this was the most thrilling ever.

Every department of the company has mapped out dynamic plans for broad expansion and for product and service improvement that is nothing less than wonderful. There is no question in my mind that this will be the greatest year in our history.

I'm not talking about sales alone.

You'll get a detailed report next week of the many things that are either ready to go, or are in process and will be ready soon. You'll see a dozen reasons why our national image, public confidence and dealer acceptance will take a missile-like thrust upward in the coming months.

You'll see why you'll be prouder than ever to represent the company and how your personal income will boom.

It would have made more sense to send this letter with the full report, but the news was too good to hold. I want to share it with you now.

You'll see.

My best . . .

In Summary . . . .

When preparing letters of praise, or letters intended to generate enthusiasm, you'll accomplish your objectives more certainly if you . . .

1. Keep such letters bright and brief.
2. Send unexpected letters of praise for consistent production.
3. Show your recognition of accomplishment when a big account is won.
4. Praise the good salesman who succeeds in saving an important account.
5. Show a contest winner that the good selling practices that helped him win can be applied throughout the year.
6. Help maintain the momentum in a prolonged contest.
7. Give recognition to sound organization.
8. Encourage men with ideas to continue to think creatively.
9. Express your appreciation for the man who demonstrates his appreciation of you.
10. Help your men to keep their enthusiasm high.
11. Create excitement about a new product to be introduced.
12. Make the granting of extra territory an exciting event.
13. Capitalize on new sales aids by sharing your ideas for their use.
14. Ensure the reading of lengthy reports with an advance letter.

19

Announcements to Customers
Salesman Support
Replies to Complaints

Announcements to customers

SALESMAN FIRED OR RESIGNED

Few letters you are called on to write require greater tact and thoughtful care than the announcement that a salesman has left your employ. Whether he was dismissed or has resigned to go with a competitor, the ice you tread is thin.

As your representative he has been calling on his accounts at regular intervals and probably has developed some close friends. If you had reason to fire him, the likelihood is that he is full of resentments and will make a mission of spreading the word about his "bad treatment." If he is going to join a competitive firm, he will be telling why he thinks that the competitor is a better firm to buy from. In either case, you are a vulnerable target and at a severe disadvantage.

The strongest ally you have is called "American sportsmanship." The man who knocks is looked at askance. The man who is generous is admired.

Under no circumstances say anything that may be interpreted as detrimental in your letter announcing a man's departure. You hired the man and you gave him your support for a period of time. You wouldn't have done so unless you saw virtues in him. Now is the time to recall those virtues despite any bitter experiences you have had with him recently.

If your former salesman is making a trip around his territory villifying you and the company, his attitude and the things he says can do him more harm than good if your letter, in contrast, pays pleasant tribute to him.

With these considerations in mind it is clear, too, that your letter must be written and mailed with maximum speed.

Dear Mr. Knott,

You'll probably be as unhappy as we are to learn that Joe Parm no longer will be representing us.

Joe is a fine man. He has won many friends in the firm and in the field. He earned respect and true affection. But in business, as in social life, the only thing that is certain is change. Joe leaves with our warmest good wishes for continued success and happiness.

Within a few days I'll be in touch with you again to announce Joe's replacement. We have been interviewing several highly qualified candidates and the moment the final selection has been made you'll have the news. Shortly after that you'll meet him in person.

In the meantime, if there is anything I can do to help and to serve you, I'll consider it a privilege.

Cordially,

Salesman Transferred or Promoted

Your letter writing job is immensely easier and more pleasant when you tell customers that the man who has been serving them has earned and been given a promotion. Although some of the customers may regret his departure, there can be no resentment and the salesman, himself, will be out there easing the transition.

Dear Mr. Hogan,

Although you'll probably miss him, I'm sure you'll be happy to know that Mike Martin has been given a well earned promotion.

My own pride in the progress he has made and my great appreciation for the help and cooperation you have given him motivated me to share the good news with you the moment it became official.

Before he leaves his present duties you will see Mike again. He'll be by to tell you of his new responsibilities and to introduce the man who will replace him.

Sincerely,

SALESMAN RETIRES

The news of a salesman's retirement will seldom be news. When a man is planning on retirement, it is a subject to dwell on when talking with friends and customers. Your announcement is a courtesy that helps pave the way for the introduction of the replacement.

Dear Mr. Price,

Pat Smith is about to retire.

We'll miss Pat, as I'm sure you will. And I'm certain that you share our hopes that his years of retirement will be long, happy and rewarding.

Before he hangs up his working clothes and picks up the fishing rod, Pat will cover his territory once more to say good-bye to his many warm friends and to introduce his replacement.

The man you'll meet when he and Pat visit you was chosen with great care and I'm sure you'll be happy to work with him. I join Pat in thanking you sincerely for the loyalty and cooperation that helped to make his career a happy and successful one.

Cordially,

SALESMAN IS ILL

When a salesman becomes ill and will not be able to serve his territory for a period of time, announcement of the situation is essential. Many of his friends will want to be kept advised of his condition and will appreciate your obvious feeling for the salesman. By pointing the way for the customers to continue to place orders with the company, you may find that orders will be even better than usual . . . the customers' way of helping their ailing friend.

Dear Mr. Gregory,

Harry Phillips, I'm sorry to report, is on the sick list.

Right now he's in the City Hospital in New City and probably will be there another week or ten days before he is permitted to go home. He's under the best of care and his family and doctors are well pleased with his progress.

While Harry is laid up, please don't hesitate to write or phone me if I can help you in any way. I'll keep you posted about his recuperation and hope that he'll be back on his feet and in his territory before too many weeks have gone by.

Cordially,

Salesman's Death

Announcing the death of your salesman calls for delicacy. You want his customers to know of his passing and, from a business standpoint, you want them to know that a replacement will be appointed and that orders can be phoned or mailed. Mixing the two is not easy. The preferable move is to write a letter that simply announces the death and, a week or two later, write a second letter on the business aspects.

The letter to Mr. Embrey, however, is one means of combining the two in a way that is not offensive.

Dear Mr. Embrey,

It is with heavy heart that I pass along the news that Myron Tait has passed away.

I know that you will miss him as will those of us who knew and worked with Myron all these years. He was a man who attracted true affection and respect.

We will, of course, take steps to find a well qualified man to pick up where Myron left off. In the meantime I'll do my best to be helpful to you in any way I can. Please write or phone if there is anything I can do for you.

Sincerely,

Introducing a New Man

The letter below not only introduces a new man, but sells him as a warm human being . . . a man people would want to meet and know. You will have opportunities to extend a letter of this type in many cases. Details of a new man's former affiliations and experience can add strength to the letter if they are appropriate and make the salesman sound interesting and valuable.

Dear Mr. Bice,

Just a short time ago I wrote to tell you that we were in the process of selecting a new man to serve your territory. Now, I'm delighted to tell you, the choice has been made.

Paul Barns will call on you within the next ten days to introduce himself. Of the various candidates we interviewed, Paul was our unanimous choice. He's a warm, intelligent man with a splendid experience that will be of value to you. He's a man with ideas.

When he drops in I hope you'll have the time to have a good talk with him so that you'll see the fine qualities we did. You'll like Paul.

Cordially,

Salesman Support

There are many letters you can send to a salesman's customers that will be helpful to him. Not only do such letters make him more welcome when he calls, but they serve to portray your own company as "nice people to deal with."

Special Event in Salesman's Life

Whether it is a special birthday, wedding, anniversary or special recognition by the firm, a letter that invites a salesman's customers to join in commemoration of the event will get a warm reception from customers and will serve as a lasting boost to the salesman's morale and loyalty to the company.

Dear Mr. Matting,

John Bryon doesn't know it, but I'm sending this message to his many good friends in his territory.

September . . . next month . . . is John's tenth anniversary with our company. They have been ten great years for all concerned . . . for John, for his customers, for the company.

A number of surprises have been planned for him. His fellow workers are giving him a surprise dinner when he comes off the road at the end of the month; the president of the company is giving him a special award at a special staff meeting and I'm tipping all of his customers to what is shaping up.

Please keep our plans secret and if you see any way to help make September John's all-time record month for sales, nothing would thrill him more.

Many thanks.

                                        Cordially,

Praise of Customer

The following letter to Mr. Callan can do a great deal to cement a fine relationship between salesman and customer. But it must be genuine. People sense when other people sincerely like and admire them. They are also able to sense the opposite. The Callan letter sent to a customer who does not feel that the salesman really holds him in high regard can backfire.

Dear Mr. Callan,

I just had lunch with Pete Morris.

In reviewing his most recent trip through his territory, he spent a good percentage of his time talking about you. I just thought you'd like to know how much Pete admires and respects you, your skills, intelligence and thoughtful consideration.

Sales managers so often have to listen to salesmen complaining about some of the people they serve, this was so refreshing I had to obey the impulse to share it with you.

Cordially,

New Line Information Preceding Saleman's Call

It is not unusual for a company to make a mass mailing to all customers and prospects regarding new merchandise or new advertising plans. It is unusual, however, to handle it with a personal letter tied to the desire of a customer's salesman to serve. The letter to Mr. Marx carries with it the new line story, but the big feature is the special consideration of the salesman for Mr. Marx and his best interests. Everyone benefits from a letter of this type.

Dear Mr. Marx,

Last night we concluded a three-day meeting attended by our entire field force.

But before Al drove off this morning, I promised I'd alert you to what is coming so that you'd be one of the first to know. With this letter is a reprint of an ad we'll be running in the leading national magazines starting in January. The reprint tells a big part of the new story and Al, when he sees you, will give you the background details.

My best good wishes for a record fall and winter.

Cordially,

Gratitude for a Big Order

The salesman does the selling and the salesman does the thanking when a good customer places an unusually big order. But additional thanks from you will be well received by the customer and, expressed as it is in the next letter, it enhances the salesman's relationship with the customer.

Dear Mr. Halgren,

Bob just phoned me about that handsome order you placed with him. Many thanks.

I know how much team work there has been between you and Bob and I could understand his enthusiasm for this rewarding result.

Every time a new merchandising concept has been discussed here, in the home office, Bob has always expressed his eagerness to bring the idea to you. He has a keen appreciation of your ready acceptance of new ideas and modern techniques and the size of your present order is a clear demonstration of how effective your progressiveness has been.

Let's hope that you, Bob and I will, in time, look back to today and remember it as no more than a great beginning of merchandising and selling.

Much appreciation.

Cordially,

The Salesman Was Not at Fault

When something goes wrong with the handling of a customer's order, the logical man to blame is the only man the customer knows and sees . . . the salesman. Considerations of unfairness aside, an incident of that type can weaken future dealings between customer and salesman. A letter from you, placing the blame where it belongs, can prove to be an important help to your salesman.

Just saying that the error was not the salesman's isn't enough. Your letter should bring out the fact of the salesman's concern and his appreciation of the customer.

Dear Mr. Martini,

This morning a new order was rushed to you to replace the one that was sent in error.

Most of all I want you to know that Phil was in no way responsible for the error. I checked his order and instructions and they were precisely what you wanted. The mistake took place in the shipping department.

Phil was deeply concerned when the error was uncovered. He holds you in such high regard, and appreciates your business so much, it upset him considerably to see anything go wrong with your account.

Accidents will happen, but when a man like Phil sees them happen to one of his favorite people he doesn't rest until he finds ways to avoid any duplications in the future. He has come up with a new method of double checking shipments that we have adopted. It will be a great asset to all of our customers.

Thanks for your understanding and patience.

Cordially,

Replies to Complaints

When a customer writes or phones to complain about a salesman, you are confronted with a difficult situation. If the salesman has not been guilty of anything serious enough to justify dismissal, you must give him your support and, at the same time, placate the customer and try to resell him on the man.

DISCOURTESY

The following letter to Mr. Murphey doesn't condone the discourtesy but puts it in proper perspective. It reveals the genuine concern the cause of the complaint created and spells out the actions that have been taken as a result. Mr. Murphey knows, after reading the letter, that his report of the incident was not taken lightly.

Dear Mr. Murphey,

I don't blame you for being disturbed by Bert's remarks when he was in your offices last week. Thanks for taking the time and trouble to tell me about the incident.

Bert and I had a long talk today and, I can assure you, he feels as badly about it as I do. He knows how wrong he was and, the chances are, you have heard from him by this time.

There is never any excuse for discourtesy and I offer none for Bert. My personal conviction is that overwork and worry about his wife's illness combined to make him acutely sensitive and irritable.

Both of us have seen and worked with Bert long enough to know that he's unusually pleasant and thoughtful under normal circumstances. He has great liking and respect for you.

I've encouraged him to take a two-week rest. This will give him a chance to regain his mental and physical strength and to be close to home where his mind and concerns are while his wife is ill. Happily, she's recovering nicely.

When Bert sees you again, I'm certain that he'll be the man we have always known . . . not the stranger he was last week.

Sincerely,

Not Enough Service

Service complaints call for analysis. Some are justified and some are not. If the complaint is a sound one, explaining it and giving your salesman support are not enough. It is essential that you specify the remedial steps that have been planned and will be taken. This is illustrated in the two letters that follow.

Dear Mr. Allwin,

You are right: Harvey should visit your plant more often. I appreciate your contacting me to bring the problem out in the open.

And I'll confess. It is my fault, not Harvey's.

Harvey is a fine salesman and I've been doing all I can to help him to make fullest use of his knowledge and skills . . . to reach new heights of success. Perhaps I have been too ambitious for him, prompting him to stretch himself too thin.

Your account requires constant attention and merits it. This morning Harvey and I had a long session and have worked out some changes in his schedule. You'll see the difference at once and I'm confident that you'll be well satisfied.

The happiest man of all is Harvey. He's been well aware of your need for greater attention and now he can follow his own, healthy inclinations.

                                        Cordially,

——————

Dear Mr. Quinton,

I am deeply grateful to you. You performed a great service to Charlie and to our firm by writing that thoughtful letter.

Charlie's failure to give you the service to which you are completely entitled can't be excused, even though it may, to some extent, be explained.

He is an enthusiast with tremendous drive and big ambitions. But enthusiasm sometimes wears blinders. Charlie's excited desire to bring our story to more and more people is the root of his problem. Actually, it is the root of my problem as his sales manager. I have failed to instill in him the attitude that will bring him true success.

The attitude I subscribe to . . . and the one Charlie had not embraced . . . is that customers are more important than prospects.

But, thanks to your letter, Mr. Quinton, this has changed.

Today I spent several hours with Charlie. As a result . . . and this should be gratifying to you . . . two of us learned a great deal. I learned how to impart that attitude more effectively and Charlie learned the importance of giving his good customers the service they deserve.

You'll see the difference from now on.

My sincerest thanks.

Cordially,

Misrepresentation

Who is telling the truth? When a customer accuses a salesman of having misrepresented and the salesman denies it, you are called on to be a Solomon. Presumably, you know your salesman well enough, and have trained him properly enough to accept his version of the story. And it is quite possible that the customer isn't lying, but genuinely misunderstood.

In any event, you are faced with the need to write a satisfying reply to a serious charge. You want to reinstate the good reputation of your company . . . you want to retain the customer . . . you want the salesman to be accepted.

Dear Mr. Ralph,

Years ago I learned that our greatest friends are those who speak out when they have sound reason to be unhappy. My sincere thanks for telling me about your recent unhappy experience with our representative, Owen Mason.

I was shocked when I read your letter.

It is my conviction that we have products and services that we can offer with pride. There is no room and no justification for exaggeration or misrepresentation. Even if the items we offer were not as good as they are, misstatements are, in my estimation, unforgivable and the poorest form of salesmanship.

Owen and I had a long session together and thoroughly reviewed the statements he made to you prior to your purchase. I am sure you heard him make the claims you reported. I am equally sure that Owen did not intentionally distort. His error may have resulted from an excess of enthusiasm. In any event, our talk convinced me that he is too intelligent and has too much integrity to knowingly stretch the truth.

You have returned the order and I don't blame you. Under the circumstances I would have done the same.

The tone of your letter tells me that you are a man with an open mind. Our products are good and, based on the long experience we have had supplying others in your field, I know that you can use them profitably.

It takes courage to do so, but Owen is eager to meet you again and to attempt to demonstrate to you that we can serve you to our mutual advantage. He will be phoning you to ask for an appointment. I hope you'll give him that chance.

Cordially,

In Summary . . . .

When writing letters to customers to announce changes in sales personnel, to boost salesmen or to handle customer complaints, it will help you to. . .

1. Be generous with praise when announcing the departure of a salesman.
2. Be quick to tell of a man leaving.
3. Provide full information when a man is to be on extended sick leave.
4. Handle a death announcement and any message about business with great tact.
5. Introduce a new man with a personality picture that is appealing.
6. Look for special events in a salesman's life that his customers can share.
7. When a salesman expresses genuine admiration for a customer, let the customer know about it.
8. Use individual letters, tied to the salesman, to bring customers advance news of new merchandise.
9. Join your salesman in thanking a good customer for an unusually big order.

10. If an error has been made and the salesman was not at fault, hasten to absolve the salesman.
11. Make it evident that a customer's complaint about a salesman's actions was not taken lightly.
12. If you are to retain a salesman who has irritated a customer, your reply, in part, should support your man.
13. Spell out the steps to be taken to satisfy a customer complaint.
14. Face up to a charge of misrepresentation in a manner that maintains company prestige and opens the door for the salesman to return.

20

How Your Letters Should Be Prepared and Handled

Dirty sneakers and a freshly pressed tuxedo are not a recommended combination. Nor does it pay to write a great letter and then permit it to go in the mail looking like dirty sneakers.

LITTLE THINGS COUNT

The letters you write are important . . . at least they are intended to perform some important functions for you. Failure to keep a watchful eye on detail can destroy their importance and can even cause damage.

I was in Flint, Michigan to give a talk to the local Sales and Marketing Executives Club at a dinner meeting. The president of the group sat next to me during dinner and we found that we had a great deal in common. He was the head of a local securities firm that specialized in the sale of mutual fund shares.

When I asked him what particular mutual funds he favored, he named several and added, "Last month we came close to making a change." He asked me if I knew a certain man who was the national sales manager for a very substantial group of mutual funds. I know the man well. He's a tremendous salesman and a highly effective speaker.

"Well," my dinner companion told me, "He was here last month and spent two days with me. We spent most of the first day together and I was sufficiently impressed to call a special meeting of our salesmen the following day. He talked to them for nearly two hours and did a first rate job. He won their enthusiasm and heightened my own. When the meeting ended, we went back to my office and discussed some other details. Before he left he said he would send me a letter detailing all the things we had talked over and all of the things his organization would do to help us to improve our sales in general and our sales of his funds in particular.

"A week later," he went on, "I had a three page, single-spaced letter from him." He shook his head. "You know, Ferd, there were nine glaring typographical or spelling errors in that letter. I counted them. And that killed the deal for me. I called it off. We're interested in our customers and you know how vital it is to have the details of investing handled with precision. When I saw that one of the top executives of this group was willing to tolerate such sloppiness, and obviously failed to check a letter before signing, I didn't dare do business with them."

Whether or not you agree that this man was or was not justified, is of no importance whatsoever. The story, as I told it, is absolutely true. What is so important about the story is the realization that the people we sell to . . . the people we write to . . . have the complete right to make such decisions. You and I can't say, "You can't do that. You are being unreasonable." I'm sure that the national sales manager of that fund was completely baffled by the collapse of his deal. His "almost customer" probably simply said that he'd changed his mind.

Your customers are entitled to be as arbitrary and as whimsical as they please. If they take a sloppy letter to mean that you are indifferent about them or about your work, they can and will knock you out and there is no court of appeals that you can turn to.

ALWAYS READ BEFORE YOU SIGN

No matter how much faith you have in your secretary, if you use one, don't take chances. Read before you sign. The most perfect secretary on earth is also human, and any human is capable of errors. Nor is it wise to let a seemingly small error, or a messy erasure go by in order to spare feelings or save time. Have it typed over. Too much is at stake to do less.

ANSWER LETTERS IN A HURRY

When a customer writes to you or phones to ask for something that requires a mailed reply, take instant action. Your speed in replying is an effective way of saying, "I think you are important. I respect you." Any delay in replying says the opposite. Make a point of responding to customers the same day the need arises.

A man who travels, or is out of his office for a few days, should make arrangements for the handling of customer requests and inquiries. Somebody in his office should be given the responsibility of checking his mail and messages. When the occasion calls for it a letter, similar to the one below, should be mailed.

Dear Mr. Jay,

Your letter to Mr. Henks arrived this morning.

He is out of the city now, but will be back at the office this coming Tuesday. Your letter will be on his desk and I'm sure you'll hear from him promptly.

Sincerely,

If the person doing this chore for you can give the customer any of the requested help or information, so much the better.

Your Stationery

The appearance of the letterheads and envelopes you use is important. The chances are that your firm has attractive stationery, and, if so, that is fine. You have no problem. If it looks like the whiskers of the founder, maybe some action is needed. Stationery that fails to portray efficiency, modernity and reliability can create negative impressions of you or your firm, or both. Such reactions may be conscious or subliminal. It doesn't matter. If the possibility exists, why take chances? You, as a salesman, may or may not be able to influence your company to upgrade. It is worth the try. If you fail to win your point, make a modest investment. Have some neat letterheads, envelopes and memo heads prepared for your personal use. Most printers are creative. They can help you to design the type of stationery that speaks up for you favorably.

If the nature of your work calls for a heavy volume of quick notes to customers, it may pay to look for some of the patented hurry-up communication forms on the market. They come in carbonized sets and explain themselves at the top. They tell the recipient that the form has been used to save his time. He can jot his reply in the area designated for it, put the original carrying your message and his answer in his file and mail you the carbon. When you order these sets, your name, firm name and address are imprinted on them.

While the hurry-up form is a fine and a considerate time saver for hurry-up messages, avoid using it for other types of correspondence. Using it, for example, to send birthday greetings, to talk about a new sales aid, or for anything beyond a request for or reply to the need for a simple fact or two, makes whatever you say less important than it should be.

Handwriting vs. Typing

There are times when a handwritten letter and a hand addressed envelope can be the right choice . . . but not often. It is the right choice if you are writing a letter of condolence, a get-well letter and, perhaps, a letter of congratulations. It is the right choice when you send letters or postcards to customers while on a vacation or on hotel stationery while on a business trip.

For most other letters, however, typing is preferable. Typing in most cases is easier to read and, therefore, more considerate of the reader's time. Typing is the well established and well accepted method of conducting business correspondence. Handwriting, just possibly, may impart a feeling that you or your firm can't afford secretarial help.

Finally, typing enables you to keep a file of carbons of your letters, and this can be important to you.

Who Does the Typing?

This may be no problem at all if you have a secretary, access to a secretarial pool, or the privilege of borrowing a secretary when needed. For many salesmen, however, it is a constant problem. They have to do it themselves, employ a secretarial service or . . . being salesmen . . . sell their wives on taking over.

For many types of letters there is another choice . . . a choice that may be used with economy and efficiency even by those with their own secretaries.

There are certain letters that you will want to use in quantity at one time, or will want to use consistently, over the years, whenever certain circumstances present themselves. An example of the former could be a letter to all customers conveying news of a price change, new lines, alterations, or a move you are going to make. In the latter case, it could be the letter you send to people after your first call.

In either case, you can have your letters typewritten on an automatic typewriter. The letters are just as personal in appearance, for they are, in fact, individually typed. The difference is that the letter itself is punched into a tape. A typist simply types the name, address and the "Dear ——," and the tape then activates the keys, one at a time, but with great speed, to type the text of the letter. The advantages are obvious. Not only can quantities of letters be produced rapidly, but once you have proof-read and okayed the master, you don't have to read each letter you sign. All are identical.

There are a number of machines of this type on the market, with varying degrees of flexibility. Some have paragraph selectors, so that you can order the machine to produce a variety of letters, each designed to cater to differences in your list. All of them permit the machine to stop at any point so that the operator can fill-in a name, figures, dates, or what have you. You can even punch your mailing list on tape, and some machines have the capability of doing the total typing job, including the addressing of the envelopes. Any of them can give you one or more carbon copies.

Equipment of this type is not inexpensive. Some large sales offices can easily afford the installation of a battery of automatic letter writers. In most cases, one operator is able to keep three machines going at once. But if the investment is out of proportion to the need, there are service companies that offer automatic letter writing as a regular service. Prices will vary, primarily depending on the length of the letter, but, on the average, you can figure that you can buy letters for about twenty or twenty-five cents a copy, which is considerably less than you'd pay to a secretarial service where each letter is typed manually.

Personalized or Unpersonalized Letters

There are circumstances that dictate the use of a large volume of letters, accompanied by reply cards, embracing invitations to phone, or suggestions that the prospect visit a store or office. More often than not mailings of this type are created and handled by a company and not by individual salesmen. But many salesmen elect to initiate such mailings themselves. When they do, they usually face the question of whether to personalize. . . or not to personalize.

Personalizing . . . having each letter start with "Dear Mr. Green," . . . is the most costly method. You can personalize a mass mailing by having the letters produced by the automatic equipment you just read about or by more economical methods. Or you can eliminate the personal element.

The basis for decision is purely economics. Two factors must be weighed. Regardless of all other considerations, what you can afford to spend is basic. The other consideration is . . . what is being offered? Without a question, individually typed letters, or letters that appear to be individually typed, will produce more results than unpersonalized letters. If what you offer has a big price tag on it, even one additional response may pay the extra cost of personalizing many times over. If you offer a low cost item, personalizing probably won't be justified.

If, therefore, the cost of your mailing is insignificant in relation to the sales you might make, by all means go top drawer and have your letters typed automatically with perfect personalizations. If the sales you may make are down a few notches, but still substantial enough per sale to motivate you to pay for some personalization, you can have your letters printed and then "filled-in." One good method is to have the original typed on a carbon ribbon machine, photographed and reproduced by the photo-offset method, and then the salutations are typed in, one-by-one, on typewriters with the identical type face, also using carbon ribbon. Done professionally, the matching can be excellent. If you can't have them done professionally, skip it. A poorly done personalization is worse than none. It insults the intelligence of the reader.

And if you decide that what you sell doesn't justify the cost of any personalization, use what is called a "benefit caption" where the salutation normally appears. A benefit caption's function is to lure . . . attract . . . shock. It must do something to pull the reader into the body of the letter. Here's what a benefit caption looks like:

Don't leave town . . .

Within twenty-four hours you are going to . . . and so on into the heart of the text.

Nothing Stands Still

If you use certain letters regularly and simply order a secretary or an automatic typing service to send one of your standard letters to a new list, make a practice of reading your standard letters not less than once a month. It is all too easy to prepare a group of standard letters and then forget what they say. Times change, conditions change, circumstances change. If your letters don't reflect those changes, you may cause yourself some problems and embarrassment.

There is another reason to subject your standard letters to regular reviews. When you created the letters, you were satisfied that they were as clear and as effective as you could make them. In the process of reviewing them each month, however, inescapably, you will begin to recognize the desirability of making some improvements. After a period of use, you'll have learned that one letter hasn't been bringing the results or reactions you thought it would. Clearly, there is need to give the letter more power, perhaps a whole new approach. In another letter you'll be startled to see that you could be misunderstood because of the way you stated something. When you first wrote it, the expression seemed crystal clear. But now you are looking at it with a fresh viewpoint and the error is shocking.

From many viewpoints the review is essential.

The Question of Enclosures

You just received a supply of provocative new folders describing one of your company's products. Should you enclose one with each letter you send to customers and prospects? It does seem like a good idea. The folder will ride along free . . . no extra postage, envelope or addressing. It may arouse interest in the product and lead to a sale. It gives your customers additional information about the product. There are many plusses.

But wait. Think about the nature of the letter you are mailing. Is it a letter that's important in your eyes? Do you want to do everything possible to be certain that it gets the full and direct attention of the man to whom it is addressed? Do you want him to dismiss everything else from his mind while considering what you have said?

Professional creators of mail order and direct mail advertising will use every device they can think of to make their mass mailings look like individual business letters. More often than not they have no choice other than to include a circular and a reply form. They wish they didn't have to because they know that anything that rides with a letter . . . any printed piece as opposed to a typed letter, or the facsimile of a typed letter . . . shouts advertising.

Before you make up your mind that you want to enclose the folder, ask yourself if you might be needlessly subjecting yourself to that handicap. In many cases you'll decide that the circular won't hurt. You are writing to your old customer and good friend, Ned, and he'll read your letter even if you enclose a bushel of folders. Fine. Put the folder in. Just be sure to weigh the pros and cons before making the decision.

The folder may even prompt you to mail them to all of your list because you consider it to be a highly effective selling tool. By all means follow through with that idea. But don't send it out alone. Picture yourself as the invited guest speaker at a dinner meeting. You are unknown to the audience. Dinner is over and the chairman nudges you and says, "All right. Get up and start talking."

Not only would you feel naked and ill at ease getting up without introduction or fanfare, but the audience would be equally uncomfortable. They would have no basis for accepting you or what you said.

If you decide to mail a company folder, send along a covering letter. The letter is the chairman making the introduction and telling why it will pay to read and heed the folder. The letter doesn't have to be elaborate. It can be a simple memo like this:

Dear Harry,

Take a moment to read the enclosed folder. It has some valuable facts that can serve you well.

Regards,

The memo, or letter, not only motivates the reader to read, but serves to keep you and your personality in the picture . . . and that's important to you.

Putting It in the Mail

Right down to the finish line, little things count. You write letters to busy people, and the more you do to make them easy to read, the more likely they are to be read.

Fold your letters so that the letterhead and the opening of the letter are visible. Letters frequently are folded over and over, with all the text enclosed and out of sight. If they are visible and facing the back flap of the envelope, the moment the envelope is opened reading is possible, even while the letter is being lifted out. People open envelopes with the back flap facing them, in most cases. That's why your letter should be inserted in that manner.

Even the postage you use can help.

Metered mail is a great economy when a company turns out great quantities of mail. We're accustomed to seeing metered mail on our desks and in our homes. It is completely acceptable and efficient. But if you are making every effort to win particular attention to a letter you are mailing, go to the trouble of buying commemorative stamps for it. They are big and they usually are handsome and eye catching. They call attention to your letter. If you are sending it air mail, take a red pen and write AIR MAIL on it in big bold letters. That makes it look important.

In Summary . . . .

How your outgoing mail is prepared and handled can have an important influence on how it is received. Keep these factors in mind:

1. Read before you sign.
2. Don't compromise on small errors or sloppy corrections.
3. Answer inquiries the day you get them.
4. If you travel, arrange to have letters acknowledged at once.
5. The stationery you use should be attractive and up-to-date.
6. Handwriting is fine for strictly personal messages, but business letters should be typed.
7. If secretarial help is a problem, investigate an automatic letter writing service.
8. There are several factors to weigh when deciding whether or not to personalize mailings to your entire list.

9. Give all standard letters a monthly review.
10. Think twice before putting folders in with your letters.
11. If mailing a folder, always include a covering letter.
12. Make the little elements . . . folding, inserting and postage . . . work for you.